The Work of the Motion Picture Cameraman

LIBRARY OF FILM AND TELEVISION PRACTICE

THE WORK OF THE FILM DIRECTOR
A. J. Reynertson

THE WORK OF THE SCIENCE FILM MAKER
Alex Strasser

THE WORK OF THE INDUSTRIAL FILM MAKER
John Burder

THE WORK OF THE TELEVISION JOURNALIST
Robert Tyrrell

The Work of the Motion Picture Cameraman

FREDDIE YOUNG
PAUL PETZOLD

Preface by
Sir Michael Balcon

FOCAL PRESS
London & New York

ISBN 0 240 50766 5

First published 1972
Second Impression 1975

Printed and bound in Great Britain by
Richard Clay (The Chaucer Press), Ltd.,
Bungay, Suffolk

Contents

Preface

BY SIR MICHAEL BALCON

IF I WERE writing Freddie Young's biography, it would probably be titled "The Man Who Had No Ambition to Become a Film Director." It is said that most men are failures insomuch as achievement so often falls short of aspiration; not so Freddie who set out to become a cinematographer—and a creator of visual images. Freddie has not only achieved his ambition but in so doing became the top man of his profession in this country. There are many who think he has few superiors in the world and consequently those who are to follow us in the years to come are fortunate that he has written in collaboration with Paul Petzold a detailed account of his identification with feature film production.

Five years before the turn of the century the first motion pictures were made; a year before I was born and some seven years before the birth of Freddie Young and our life-cycles are to all intents and purposes the life-cycle of films. It is remarkable that Freddie who is some years my junior—and has been a friend of mine for forty years—has worked in the film industry for fifty-five years whereas I have been going for a mere half a century.

He started work in the Gaumont laboratory at Lime Grove, Shepherds Bush at the age of fifteen and by virtue of his basic training and his subsequent work he has known and experienced every important technological development in film making that has taken place in the twentieth century.

When Freddie moved from the laboratory to the studio floor, open arcs were in common use and eyesight protection was the order of the day; cameras were cranked by hand; artists wore heavy make-up. He has experienced the change from orthochromatic to panchromatic film, has bridged the gap from silent films to sound and switched from black-and-white to colour.

The introduction of sound was something of a punishment for

cameramen. Professor Thorold Dickinson in his recent book *A Discovery of Cinema* says "the banal ways to apply sound to the silent film were either to make silent films with a sound track of music and effects or to make a film record of a stage production. For the latter they set up four or five cameras, each loaded with ten minutes of film in clumsy sound-proof booths (from which the cameramen sometimes fell out after ten minutes in a dead faint)." Freddie must have been engaged on many such films in the early days of sound. He has also coped with expanding screens of varying ratios without compromising effective groupings and pictorial composition.

I do not propose to give details of all the films with which Freddie has been identified as full information is available in the book proper: suffice it to say that he has worked with directors and producers whose names are known throughout the world. They include inter alia Herbert Wilcox to whom Freddie was contracted for so many years, Carol Reed, Michael Powell, Victor Saville, George Cukor, David Lean, Richard Brooks, Vincente Minnelli, John and Roy Boulting, Sam Woods, Joseph Mankiewicz, Walt Disney and Sam Spiegel.

The fundamental conception in major films is rare and it follows that these films are a group effort in much the same way as ballet, and I have no doubt that the directors and/or producers with whom Freddie has been associated would happily testify that his contribution to the artistic merits of the resultant films has often been equal to their own. The films with David Lean include *Lawrence of Arabia, Doctor Zhivago* and *Ryan's Daughter*. Need I say more!

It has to be admitted that most of the films of the great American era were largely escapist and divorced from life. Settings of Arabian Nights opulence peopled largely by gorgeous males and females, the latter having to be photographed in close-up against backgrounds often divorced from the film proper. The cameraman of today (as a result of British and European influences) has to be completely involved and concerned with mood and atmosphere and it is here that Freddie's genius emerges—the choking sand and dust of the desert; the chill and horror of the Steppes of Russia; the dramatic scenes to which more than one dimension has been added by a brilliant photographic interpretation. Freddie Young paints in light!

Our paths are intertwined. In the early 1930s I took over the re-built studios in Lime Grove, Shepherds Bush and the old laboratories where Freddie Young started his career and we had been concerned in several films together. Some years later, in 1936, Freddie, Victor Saville and I became involved with the foundation of Metro-Goldwyn-Mayer British Studios Ltd. and an exciting programme which included *Yank at Oxford, Good-bye Mr. Chips* (photography by Freddie) and *The Citadel*. The War came and we went our separate ways.

Film-makers are given to the use of superlatives; in writing about Freddie Young it is difficult to avoid them because they happen to be justified. No recital of the international awards he has won could suggest a proper assessment of his work. Those who were present at the Awards Celebration arranged by the Society of Film and Television Arts or the many who saw the ceremony on television will not forget the deep throated roar of approval on the announcement that Freddie Young was to be the second Fellow of the Association; Alfred Hitchcock was the first. The acclaim was not only for his work but was also a tribute to a gentle, modest artist who enjoys the affection and respect of his fellow workers.

The Work of the Motion Picture Cameraman should be widely read. For the National Film School, The Royal College of Art, The London School of Film Technique and other training centres in this country and the United States of America a study of the book should be a compulsory exercise. There should also be a wider public for the story of a completely successful and rewarding working life which happily continues.

Introduction

WHEN MR A. KRASZNA-KRAUSZ—the Managing Director of Focal Press—suggested a few years ago that I should write a book on motion picture photography, I agreed to try to do something about it. At that time I was very busy shooting a film and I realized the difficulty would be to find the time to write. After a hard day's work in the studio or on location, one arrives home tired and with very little inclination to spend the evening working on a book about filming.

Paul Petzold, of Focal Press, was going to collaborate with me on the book, so it became a habit that Paul would come to dinner at my flat and the rest of the evening would be spent with a tape recorder, answering his questions until about 11 o'clock when Paul would have to dash to catch the last tube train back to his flat in Hampstead.

After a few weeks of this routine, I had to go abroad to start another film, *Doctor Zhivago* directed by David Lean for whom I had also photographed *Lawrence of Arabia*. This involved nine months shooting and just before the end of filming, my wife was rushed off to the British American Hospital where she gave birth to our son David who, being born two months prematurely, spent some weeks in an incubator. Another few weeks passed before we were allowed to fly him home, so there was quite an additional delay before Paul and I could resume our collaboration.

Once home, we had a few months hard work together while I was making a film for Sidney Lumet, *The Deadly Affair*, in London. Then followed *You Only Live Twice* (directed by Lewis Gilbert) for which I had to go to Japan for two months. However, as the rest of the film was shot in England we made considerable progress.

But then came *The Battle of Britain* (directed by Guy Hamilton). This involved a location in Spain which was to represent German occupied France—the reason for this being that the Spanish Air Force owned many of the World War II German Messerschmitts and Heinkels. As the Spanish aircrews were very expert at flying these planes it was the obvious thing to have them do so. Then we returned to England for the British airfield sequences with the Spitfires and Hurricanes.

That summer in England was dreadfully wet and as the real "Battle" of 1940 was fought out over a few weeks of marvellous summer weather we were considerably delayed as we chased from Duxford to North Weald, then to Debden and to Hawkinge waiting for the sun to appear. On my return to the studios for the interior work, Paul and I continued working on the book in the evenings.

The next interruption was *Ryan's Daughter*, again with David Lean, which took me to Ireland for over a year. And again a very wet period which put us considerably behind schedule and even necessitated a trip to South Africa for some sunny beach scenes.

On my return Paul and I had our final sessions and when I had to leave for Spain to film *Nicholas and Alexandra* (for Sam Spiegel and Franklin Schaffner) my good friend and associate cameraman Bob Huke very kindly read through the book. I am indebted to him for his inspiration and help in checking our information and assisting with the diagrams.

As a result of these frequent interruptions the book has taken several years to complete and may reflect that in its coverage of certain aspects.

Our next problem was to find suitable photographs to illustrate the book. I had collected a number of stills which the stills cameraman had kindly given me when working on various pictures, but these mainly featured the director and camera crews and Focal Press were keen to have stills which would illustrate the different types of working situation and the lighting which I had used to express mood or dramatic effect.

Now the stills man's job is to shoot pictures for publicity purposes and for exhibition outside the cinemas. These pictures are not the same shape or format as that of the movie camera so they do not give the huge wide screen effect of Panavision in contemporary cinemas. Anybody who has watched films made for the wide screen on TV knows how much is lost even there—plus the fact that most stills are shot in black and white and so are not really representative of the lighting for the screen. So I'm afraid the stills are not really what I would have liked to have to illustrate the book, but I am told that they still reflect something of the pictorial flavour of my work. The reader may be a better judge of that than I.

For what it is worth, and based on more than fifty years experience in the film industry, I have tried to give the reader some basic understanding of the problems of the motion picture photographer, together with the working conditions and the artistry of lighting for mood and dramatic effect, combined with problems of the budget for making the film, and the facts about working with a team of people, possibly numbering up to two hundred on a large picture.

Usually, there is quite a friendly atmosphere and comradeship plus a bit of rivalry and jockeying for position. When the picture is falling behind schedule there may be some tension and possibly bad tempers flying around. But the majority of people concerned are very experienced and they are all very aware of the fact that bickering and quarrelling will get them nowhere. So sanity returns, peace prevails and everybody concentrates on finishing the picture. When it's finished and the goodbyes are said it is quite sad. Sometimes it may be years before the same people meet up again on another picture, when the excitement of joining together to start a new venture is quite an occasion.

I hope that the old hands who may read this book will understand and forgive the shortcomings and that the newcomers may glean a bit of useful knowledge from its pages.

Freddie Young
February 5th 1972

*   *   *

Acknowledgments

The authors wish to express their thanks for assistance with information to Mr David Samuelson of Samuelson Film Service Ltd., Mole Richardson (England) Ltd., and for the supply of photographs to Metro-Goldwyn-Mayer Inc., Columbia Pictures Corp. Ltd., and United Artists Corp. Ltd., and the *Sunday Times Magazine* for permission to base the diagram on page 35 on a drawing which appeared in it.

Freddie Young, O.B.E.

Born London October 9th 1902.

Entered Film Industry 1917, Gaumont Film Studios, Laboratory section. 1918 studio assistant, then second cameraman; assistant cameraman in studio until 1927.

1929–1939 with Herbert Wilcox, British and Dominions Film Corporation Ltd as director of photography.

1939–1940 Freelance director of photography.

1940–1943 Captain in army: chief cameraman and director of army training films. Invalided out of army 1943.

1944–1959 Chief cameraman for M.G.M.

1959 onwards, freelance director of photography.

Member of:
> Academy of Motion Picture Arts and Sciences, Hollywood.
> British Society of Cinematographers.
> Hon. Fellow Royal Photographic Society.
> Fellow Society of Film and Television Arts.
> Fellow British Kinematograph, Sound and Television Society.
> Hon. Member of the Association of Cinematograph Television and Allied Technicians.

Awards:
> Three Oscars—*Lawrence of Arabia, Doctor Zhivago, and Ryan's Daughter.*
> Nominated Oscars—*Ivanhoe* and *Nicholas and Alexandra.*
> Three Golden Cameras (as three Oscars) British Society of Cinematographer's Award.

Golden Globe for *Lawrence of Arabia.*
Prix d'Honneur for *Lawrence of Arabia.*
N.B.C. Emmy 1960/1961 for *Macbeth* on U.S. colour T.V. (half
U.S., half U.K. financed production of *Macbeth* in colour for
N.B.C.—the award was for the American version).
Order of the British Empire—June 1970.

The Films of Freddie Young

Victory 1918; first picture as chief cameraman 1927;

A Peep Behind the Scenes; *The Speckled Band*; *Goodnight Vienna*; *The Loves of Robert Burns*; *The King of Paris*; *White Cargo* (first talkie in England); *Rookery Nook*; *A Cuckoo in the Nest*; *Canaries Sometimes Sing*; *A Night Like This*; *Plunder*; *Thark*; *On Approval*; *Mischief* Dir./Prod. Herbert Wilcox for British and Dominions

Return of the Rat Dir. Graham Cutts, Prod. Gainsborough Pictures

The Happy Ending; *Yes, Mr. Brown*; *This'll Make you Whistle*; *That's a Good Girl*; *Nell Gwynne*; *Peg of Old Drury*; *The Little Damozel*; *Bitter Sweet*; *The Queen's Affair* Prod. Herbert Wilcox for British and Dominions

Sport of Kings; *A Warm Corner*; *The W Plan* Dir./Prod. Victor Saville

Victoria the Great Prod. Herbert Wilcox for British and Dominions

Sixty Glorious Years (Colour) Prod. Herbert Wilcox for British and Dominions

Goodbye Mr Chips Dir. Sam Wood (Freddie Young lent to M.G.M. 1937)

Nurse Edith Cavell (shot in Hollywood) Dir./Prod. Herbert Wilcox

The 49th Parallel Dir. Michael Powell. Co-prod. Michael Powell and Emeric Pressburger

Contraband Dir./Prod. Michael Powell

Busman's Honeymoon Dir. Arthur Woods for M.G.M.

The Young Mr Pitt Dir. Carol Reed for Gaumont British

Army Training Films

Caesar and Cleopatra Dir. Gabriel Pascal for United Artists

Escape Dir. Mervyn LeRoy for M.G.M.

So Well Remembered Dir. Edward Dmytryk for R.K.O.

Edward, My Son Dir. George Cukor for M.G.M.

The Conspirator Dir. Victor Saville for M.G.M.

The Winslow Boy Dir. Anthony Asquith for British Lion

Calling Bulldog Drummond Dir. Victor Saville for M.G.M.

Ivanhoe Dir. Richard Thorpe for M.G.M.
Knights of the Round Table Dir. Richard Thorpe for M.G.M.
Mogambo Dir. John Ford for M.G.M.
Invitation to the Dance Dir. Gene Kelly for M.G.M.
Bhowani Junction Dir. George Cukor for M.G.M.
The Barretts of Wimpole Street Dir. Sidney Franklin for M.G.M.
The Little Hut Dir. Mark Robson for M.G.M.
Indiscreet Dir. Stanley Donen for Warner
I Accuse Dir. José Ferrer for M.G.M.
Inn of the Sixth Happiness Dir. Mark Robson for 20th Century Fox
Solomon and Sheba Dir. King Vidor for United Artists
Betrayed Dir. Gottfried Reinhardt
Island in the Sun 20th Century Fox
Treasure Island Walt Disney
Lust for Life Dir. Vincente Minelli for M.G.M.
Macbeth Dir./Prod. George Schaefer
Greengage Summer Dir. Lewis Gilbert for Columbia
Lawrence of Arabia Dir. David Lean, Prod. Sam Spiegel for Columbia
Seventh Dawn Dir. Lewis Gilbert, Prod. Charles Feldman for United
    Artists
Lord Jim Dir. Richard Brooks for Columbia
The Deadly Affair Dir. Sidney Lumet for United Artists
Doctor Zhivago Dir. David Lean for M.G.M.
You Only Live Twice Dir. Lewis Gilbert, Prod. Harry Salzman and
    Albert Broccoli for United Artists
The Battle of Britain Dir. Guy Hamilton, Prod. Harry Salzman and
    Benny Fisz for United Artists
Ryan's Daughter Dir. David Lean, Prod. Havelock Allan and Roy
    Stevens for M.G.M.
Nicholas and Alexandra Dir. Franklin Schaffner, Prod. Sam Spiegel for
    Columbia

1

The Film Makers

THIS BOOK IS about the director of photography, or lighting cameraman as he used to be called. His job is to produce the best photographic record that can be made of the production he is engaged to work on. He plans the filming, lights it and shoots it.

His most important attributes are a fully developed pictorial sense and a sound understanding of the technical basis on which it must be built. He is an artist, and a technician.

But it is not enough for him simply to execute his job to his own satisfaction. Technical and artistic perfection cannot be achieved by one individual when his work is so dependent upon, and interwoven with, that of other people.

THE CAMERAMAN

The cameraman stands at the natural confluence of the two main streams of activity in the production of a film—where the imagination meets the reality of the film process.

Imagination is represented by the director, who in turn is heir to the ideas of the scriptwriter, as he is to those of the original author of the story. Three minds, and three contributing sources of imagination have shaped the film before the cameraman can begin to visualize it as a physical entity.

Technical reality is represented by the capabilities, availability and physical limitations of the equipment and materials the cameraman must use, as well as the size and location of the place he must work in. The requirements of the technical staff concerned with recording the sound must also be reckoned with. The problems of those controlling special effects and people with particular skills brought in to fly an aeroplane or perform a stunt can also create technical limitations.

To reconcile the often conflicting forces of the artistic and the mechanical yet maintain a good working relationship with those whose

ideals he must respect, is a primary requirement of his position. This is
the climate he works in, and it is there all the time. His own ideas must
take root here, and in fact an atmosphere that constantly poses new
problems often acts as a stimulant and a catalyst to his own artistic
vision and technical resourcefulness.

His importance

There has been a tendency in the past for some directors to attach
small importance to the photography in film making. But anyone who
has paid attention in recent years to the remarks of people in an audience
as they leave the cinema knows well enough that today's public is a
highly picture-conscious one.

Put at its lowest, good cinematography serves to give an accurate
rendering of the production that a director has prepared for the cameras.
But what if the feelings he has tried to put over are lost in the filming
stage? Or if the cameraman's approach to a scene is, if anything, producing the opposite impression to the one intended? The influence of the
camera on what happens in a film is so strong that, carelessly used, it
can, by implication at least, infuse quite another feeling or meaning
into a scene. The destructive effect on a story can easily be imagined.

It is important that the cameraman be as well-informed and involved as possible at all stages, and that he of all people should be able
to work hand-in-glove with a director. That director can then fulfil his
intentions and those of the financial backers who expect good value
from the people they have entrusted with the film.

His job

The two main responsiblities of a cameraman are the lighting of a
scene and the operation of the camera. But he has many other responsi-
bilities besides these and in order to carry them out he has a small team
of assistants—the camera crew.

Usually the cameraman is brought in first at the very early stages
of the film—the pre-production conference—to help in planning the
shooting. His advice may have a considerable bearing on the economics
as well as the practical possibilities of the production programme.

When the time comes for the production to be put on the floor, and
shooting to commence, the cameraman must take charge of the lighting,
the positioning or movement of the camera, the composition of the
picture, the exposure and the use of any special optics or film materials.

His working procedure usually goes like this. When the set is more
or less complete he gives instructions to the electricians to position the
main lights in accordance with a plan he has worked out beforehand.
This lighting scheme is designed to create or accentuate the mood
required for the scene.

Next, with the set completed, the actors are brought on for re-hearsals. The cameraman watches them closely and checks that his lighting set up is satisfactory for the action. He makes any adjustments necessary.

Now he must position the camera to give the best composition for the shot, suggesting any special camera movement that might improve it, or carrying out such movements as are asked of him. At this stage he may have to sort out several problems of lighting where a lamp may have to be moved during a shot or another repositioned because of an unwanted shadow, perhaps from some piece of studio equipment.

Following the first rehearsal he may have to ask actors to change their position or modify a movement in some way to improve or correct the scene. Additionally, he must check the effect of his lighting on the appearance of the actors.

Another rehearsal now takes place but this time the cameraman watches through the camera, checking the movement of the composition with the movement that he has planned for the camera. At this point he can see the whole effect.

Finally, after a third rehearsal where any last minute adjustments or improvements are made, the scene is shot. This is a first try and may not prove successful. Several attempts may be made before a good result is obtained.

That is, of course, only an outline of the cameraman's job. Many films take him to outdoor locations, often to remote places, where he must secure his effects using the natural elements, or a combination of natural and artificial effects. So he must know how to create convincing sunshine shots on a dull day, how to film rain, snow or what-have-you effects and operate the camera under a very wide range of conditions, in all climates, at all altitudes, at sea, in the air or on terra-firma. For equipment, he may be using anything from a small camera held in the hand, to a large wide-screen system camera mounted on a motorized crane the size of a double-decker bus. He may be providing additional illumination from the sky with a small silver-surfaced reflector, or from the power house or generators with a vast battery of powerful lights.

The cameraman's job is a far-reaching one requiring a thorough knowledge of the whole process of how a film is made. As shooting proceeds the cameraman issues instructions to the laboratories who process and print the film so that they can do it in such a way that the moods or colour values of the scenes are preserved or accentuated. Only when he has seen the finalized versions of each scene can he know that the film is ready to pass completely out of his hands into those of the editor.

The Camera Crew

The cameraman has a basic crew of three assistants, the operator, the focus puller and the clapper loader. Additionally there is often a dolly pusher, and also two non-technical people who help move the heavy equipment about. They are known as grips and in fact grips are employed for many such heavy duties around the studio or on location.

Operator

The operator is the senior member of the crew. He is the person who actually operates the camera, lines it up ready for the shot and carries out the camera movements in accordance with the cameraman's wishes. He pushes the button that starts the camera rolling and checks that the camera is running at the proper speed when the shot begins.

During rehearsals he checks that focus is correct for the particular shot, operates the zoom control if it is needed, makes sure that the right lens is in position and either lines the camera up in a suitable composition or copies the composition decided upon by the cameraman.

The cameraman moves the camera only during rehearsal when both he and the operator can look through the viewfinder together. Thenceforward each time the shot is rehearsed the operator does the movement following the moving composition correctly. If there is a dolly shot, he instructs the dolly pusher as to how to make the movement.

The operator is responsible for making sure the camera is quite operational and ready to run before each shot. He checks with the other crew members that all their jobs have been done.

In the event of illness the operator may occasionally step in to take over from the cameraman. He may also be put in charge of a second camera unit when an extra unit is needed to film subsidiary material.

Focus puller

The principal occupation of a focus puller is to set the focus of the camera lens at the correct distance for the shot, and to make any adjustments to it necessary between or during takes. This leaves the operator free to make the camera movements, and in any case on the larger cameras the operator could not alter focus and control the camera adequately at the same time.

The focus puller is told what is to be the point of focus in the scene (not necessarily the subject) and sets the lens. He takes measurements with a tape unless it is a long-range subject. During tracking shots he often uses measurements chalked on the floor. He cannot *see* the effect of the lens focus but goes by the figures engraved on the lens.

It is also the focus puller's job to place each loaded magazine on the camera, and thread the film through the camera mechanism. He makes absolutely sure that the interior of the camera is dust-free, and he frequently cleans it out. The smallest speck of grit in the camera mechanism could spoil a whole sequence, or possibly an entire day's work.

His other jobs are to change lenses, set the aperture given him by the cameraman (and the focal length, if it is a zoom lens), keep the lenses clean and attach any filters or special lenses required for a shot.

During rehearsal his focus movements are practised, and checked by the cameraman and operator. His particular skill is to translate actual distance into figures on the lens which he watches all the time.

In an emergency the focus puller would take over from the operator.

Clapper loader

The "loader" part of his title is self-explanatory. He loads the film magazines first and sometimes fits them onto the camera. He checks that there is enough footage of film remaining in the magazine in use to cover the next shot. If not, he quickly interchanges that magazine with another which he has loaded beforehand. He notes the footage of film remaining unused in the magazine on a record card which is attached to the side of the magazine with a piece of tape. He loads the magazine in darkness, in a dark room or caravan, or perhaps he may do it in a special light-tight changing bag which can be used in daylight. He also keeps a log of the footages shot, on a camera sheet. This information goes to the processor together with the film which he has unloaded from the magazines and placed in light-tight tins.

If a clapper board (page 237) is used for synchronizing sound with picture the clapper loader operates it at the beginning of each shot. He marks up the scene number in chalk on a camera slate and alters the take number before each take.

Other production details that are not actually painted onto the slate he chalks up as well. At the beginning of each shot he holds the slate in front of the lens to identify the shot for those concerned with it afterwards.

Both he and the focus puller are expected to carry some of the equipment about, although the camera grips do much of it.

Dolly pusher

If the camera is mounted on a dolly, someone who knows the technique can push the dolly in just the way required for a particular shot. He must be able to propel it at a steady rate, gather or lose speed at any point and stop or start without a jolt. The camera must travel the distance to a predetermined position and no further. Dolly pushing is not as easy as it sounds!

The various forms of motorized camera mounting widely used in the industry need to be controlled just as accurately as the simple dolly.

With cranes there are greater problems. The camera is out on an adjustable boom which also must be operated. For the more elaborate camera mountings several extra crew members are needed. As they are not needed for the regular camera work they are brought in only when this equipment is being used.

THE PERSONAL QUALITIES OF A CAMERAMAN AND HIS OPERATOR

The cameraman's life is a hard one but the very hard work is rewarding. To withstand the physical strain of long hours and to remain mentally alert all the time he needs energy and must keep fit and well. This enables him to keep up the pace, and the pace is tremendous in making a film.

The job demands working at high speed and cameramen can earn a reputation for being fast and certain, or slow and unreliable. Naturally this has a considerable bearing on a director's choice of cameraman for his next picture. Good results must be combined with a good working speed. A cameraman's eyesight needs to be good—with or without glasses. Spectacles do not matter on the camera because the eyepiece can be adjusted to suit individual sight.

Apart from learning the job, which is obviously essential, the cameraman needs to be able to exercise considerable tact and persuasion. He is often required to explain his point of view on the most subtle and elusive things in a scene and to be confident that his contentions will prove right in the end. Those ultimately responsible for the production will then appreciate the value of his advice and experience and be far more favourably disposed toward his ideas.

The most valuable personal quality in an operator is a pleasant manner. This really applies to any branch of production. Someone with an awkward personality will get nowhere. In this rather tough business, no one wants to work with a short-tempered, miserable or irritable person. The ideal man is someone likeable, diligent and hard-working. He is alert and always where he is wanted. He must be punctual in arrival and free from illness—he simply cannot afford to fall ill. In emergencies there should be someone to take over from him, but few people stay at home because of illness if they are important personnel on the floor. Colds are rather shared around the studio than kept at home. A cameraman would almost have to be unconscious not to come to work!

CREW REPLACEMENT AND PROMOTION

On occasions when the operator is absent for a few hours only, the focus puller would probably step in to take over. The clapper loader would thus change to focus puller and another clapper loader be taken on. That is why in the structure of a camera crew each member should be capable of taking over from the other. For as long as they are in one another's positions they are paid the appropriate rate for that day. For longer-term arrangements another operator would be engaged but the cameraman, knowing that the focus puller was experienced enough might consider it time he had a break and give him the job. This is probably the opportunity he has been waiting for. If a member of the unit who has been moved up proves his ability, then illness or accident may again offer him an opportunity on some future occasion. Perhaps for another film when the established operator is not available the cameraman might consider the focus puller as the operator for the whole film. This is the way people in the industry gain promotion but in point of fact they normally have quite a few years' experience in each job before moving up to the next.

Promotion is a slow process. There are very few lighting cameramen in the business who have not been at it for at least ten years and there are very few operators who have not also been focus pullers for at least five or six years. Others have been operators for twenty years and wish to remain so. They would rather work within what they feel is the limit of their capabilities and are better off without the responsibility that goes with a higher position. There are, of course, those in between, who feel that they can do the higher job and are aggrieved that they have never been given the opportunities. Somehow the opportunity comes if you are capable.

The cameraman in choosing his team should take particular care whether the men selected will be suitable for one another's jobs in the event of a mishap, especially if he is doing an important film and is going abroad. They may pass through some hazardous places where the chances of illness or accident are greater than normal.

Working together

A potential operator has to have a natural talent and feel for camera movement. He must be able to feel inside himself the mood of a scene. The camera should be controlled with a silky movement that the audience is not aware of; it floats from one good composition to another. A nervous operator who has no sense of flow produces jerky pans that do not coincide with the actors' movements and may end the scene in a bad composition with too much or too little headroom.

The movement and composition is calculated and rehearsed beforehand and agreed by the cameraman with the director. Although the operator is merely carrying out something which has been agreed, once the movement starts he is responsible for it and he has to carry it out well. The operator may certainly express opinions, but these can be overruled by the director or the cameraman who may decide their own way of doing a scene.

The director has the right to insist on doing the scene his way. However, if the operator feels that there is something wrong he should say so. Only the operator really knows if the shot is all right because he is looking through the camera at the time of shooting. He has also to instruct the dolly pusher or camera grips. For example he may need to start backing gradually and speed up at a certain point, and during the rehearsal he finds that it must be slowed down a little more gently toward the end of the movement. The camera grip repeats the movement in rehearsal until the operator tells him it is right.

Everybody is really subservient to the film as a whole—even the director has to fit in with difficulties of camera movement. He might ask for a certain movement which is either physically impossible or does not look right through the camera. If so, the operator should tell the director of photography that the way the director wants it does not work well. The director of photography would look through the camera at the initial rehearsal with the operator to see for himself. If necessary he would tell the director that what he was asking was not possible. A good director values the advice of his camera crew and would agree to change the shot in this case.

THE PEOPLE HE WORKS WITH

Director

The director is the person who turns a script into a screen story—a series of dramatized scenes designed to be photographed.

He plans the interpretation that is put on the script story, which is only the bare bones. He visualizes the action, the behaviour of characters and the mood that pervades the various scenes. The film becomes largely the product of his imagination—cameraman, scenic artist and actors are only vehicles to put his ideas into solid form. He has a sure sense of dramatic effect and this he applies right the way through the production of the film even to the editing stage.

The cameraman works immediately under the director and there is a constant working dialogue between them as the cameraman tries as near as is possible to put the director's ideas on film.

The director controls the actors, checks each scene by looking through the camera if necessary, decides how and when a scene should be modified and is the ultimate authority on all points of the production. He is present from the very early stages when the film is planned right through the shooting. He is there every day and probably for every scene—and up to the time when the film has been edited and the final release prints are made.

Producer

There are two different kinds of producer. The so-called *executive producer* of some years ago used to have as many as half a dozen films on his hands at any one time. Nowadays a producer is often on one film for the whole time of its production working hand-in-glove with the director. In some cases there are *director-producers* who handle both jobs themselves. In many present day films the one man who is director-producer has absolute power, and his opinion goes unquestioned. In turn he is responsible only to the head of the company who might be in another country.

Both co-producing star directors and actors today have much more freedom and responsibility than they used to. They very often work on a freelance basis and films are frequently made where a star who will probably be the leading man, is co-producer with the director. If the star has "a piece of the picture" he is financially involved and shares any profit that film may make. Generally a half-star half-businessman with this great responsibility works much harder to make a success of the film.

It is easier for a cameraman to work for one man who carries full responsibility. Working with separate director and producer, might sometimes result in two conflicting sources of influence and can be confusing for a cameraman.

When the leading actor is also the director and producer he places great reliance on the cameraman. After directing the other actors he has to join them in order to play his part, leaving only the cameraman to watch his own performance. In a way the cameraman is co-directing. After the scene has been tried the leading actor may come rushing back to the cameraman to ask how it went. A cameraman can give his views and indicate any points that he noticed, but it is not usually a very satisfactory basis on which to work. An actor-director has too much to do—he cannot stand by the camera and watch himself acting. He is, therefore, unable to judge the scenes in which he appears. Also he has too much on his mind because as well as directing the actors he has to see the rushes, supervise the editing of the picture and the dubbing of sound and music. Moreover, an actor rarely has all the qualifications necessary. As an actor himself, he may be enthusiastic to direct the scenes but it is best that he should do either one job or the other.

Production manager

The production manager makes a 'breakdown' of the script which specifies scene numbers and all the props and equipment needed for each day's work. A copy of this breakdown is issued to the head of every department together with a copy of the whole script which they always have with them. The cameraman compares his breakdown with the shooting script, going over the scene which he has to shoot the following day and thinking out the shots and the problems involved. The cameraman must decide upon the lighting required for every scene to be shot and give precise instructions to the electrician some days or weeks in advance.

Continuity clerk

Throughout the production the continuity clerk, usually a girl, makes careful notes of all the furniture, clothes, and of the positions of props and details in the scene connected with them so that this visual side of the continuity is maintained.

Art director

The art director is in charge of designing all the sets necessary for the film and even on location he is often called upon to modify the scene, usually by adding things to improve it, such as another tree or some grass where there was none.

Scenic artist

In early film days there was no art director, but a scenic artist would paint the background as one does for the stage. Film technique had its beginnings in stage methods and originally canvas flats were used which had supports at the back. If a picture was to be seen hanging on the wall a real painting was never used because the wall was canvas and a nail could not be driven into it. If a door was needed, but was in the background and did not have to open they would simply paint a door onto the flat. Later, when things became more exacting the art director had to resort to more substantial materials such as plywood and light moulding. Doors had to be practical—they had to open and shut—and when films developed further the art director was quite usually a trained architect. Sets would then be architecturally correct and he would understand about period decoration and furniture as well as structural design. Later, as the film business became a larger industry and more assistants were brought in to each department, the art director would have a permanent staff of plasterers, carpenters, metal-workers, engineers and set dressers who between them had the resources to find, hire or make anything necessary to provide the correct historical or geographical background for the film.

The art director is always personally responsible for the background and settings and may be making preparations at the location or studio several months before the picture is started. He is usually involved right up to the end of shooting. A studio has only limited space and as soon as one set has been used it has to be pulled down and another built in its place. He may still be building a new set only one day before the end of shooting.

Studio staff

Studios are generally owned by a holding company which may produce films, and also exhibit through their own chain of cinemas. But for a large part of the time the studio is sub-let to independent producers who hire floor space for a given period. Although the film may not concern the production company who own the studios, on occasion they handle the release of the film.

The independent producer engages his own directors, cameramen and a few other personnel. The art director is usually engaged for the film also, but sometimes the studio has a resident art director and the producer may decide that it is to his own advantage to use him.

TEAM/WORKING METHODS—HOW THEY WORK TOGETHER

Working hours and seasons

Film people work normal industrial hours, i.e. 8.30 am to 5.45 pm with an hour for lunch break and any overtime required after consultation with the shop steward. For location work, journey time must be allowed. A two-hour journey would mean an earlier call, say 6.30 am, and, with daylight failing at about 4.00 pm in winter time, the return journey would bring everybody back to the studios at 6.00 pm.

Films are planned as far as possible to avoid shooting through the midwinter months and the studios are least active at this time of the year. But during the summer, when many productions are under way, staff may not be so plentiful. Filming schedules try to take advantage of the seasonal change. On a long-term project, most exterior and location work might be shot before the autumn, finishing off in the studio during the early winter. Such planning has a bearing on the financial aspect of making a film.

Members of the team are forewarned of possible overtime requirements where a major set needs to be struck that day.

When abroad, they will often work to "continental hours" where they start at 11.00 am and work right through without a lunch break until 7.00 pm. The practice originated in France where artists used in films were stage actors who had to be at the theatre in the evening. Naturally, they could use these actors only during the day for filming. This is still a good idea because if you start at 11.00 am and work through continually without a lunch break you can maintain the impetus throughout the day rather than having to restart after lunch.

Regaining impetus can turn a one-hour lunch break into two hours of inactivity.

Recruiting the crew

In the film business most people work on a freelance basis and gain employment by virtue of their reputation. Very often a little team is formed and they may work together on several films. If at a later date they split up for one reason or another a cameraman may make a mental note of individuals and their abilities. He probably has in mind a number of people he would be very happy to employ again when given the chance.

A cameraman nearly always has the choice of his own crew. Even when occasionally someone else is recommended by a director who may have worked with him on a previous picture the cameraman has first choice of who is to be engaged. But in most cases the cameraman is left to get on with engaging all his own crew. If possible a cameraman prefers to have the same team on the studio floor as well, the same chief electrician for example. Of course, it does not always work out this way but there are usually half a dozen equally good people to choose from. Except on a strong recommendation nobody likes to risk taking on someone they have never worked with before.

There is an old saying in the business that your reputation is as good as your last film. That is not quite true. It is as good as your last several films. It is a fairly small industry and the top people in any particular field are well known to everyone. A cameraman rarely has any problem in selecting his crew as there is usually someone available whom he has used before, or who has earned a good reputation.

Crew/director relationship

A film is not really in any sense made by one person alone. Nevertheless, teamwork though it is, once the film is actually on the floor and shooting commences, the director leads the team and always has the last word. He, after all, carries the greatest responsibility—seeing the picture through all its stages.

The cameraman has general control over his own staff and in such a matter as seeing the rush prints of the previous day's work the director would always consent to the cameraman's crew members, his assistant cameraman and operator, being present. This is justified because the crew can clear up any technical matters and answer complaints about focus or framing. The relationship between director and other staff is so much a question of teamwork that it would be a very unhappy unit if the "boss and employee' technique were applied. No director with any sense at all would try to enforce that feeling. A director needs the friendship of the unit and although he might be rather bossy at times he

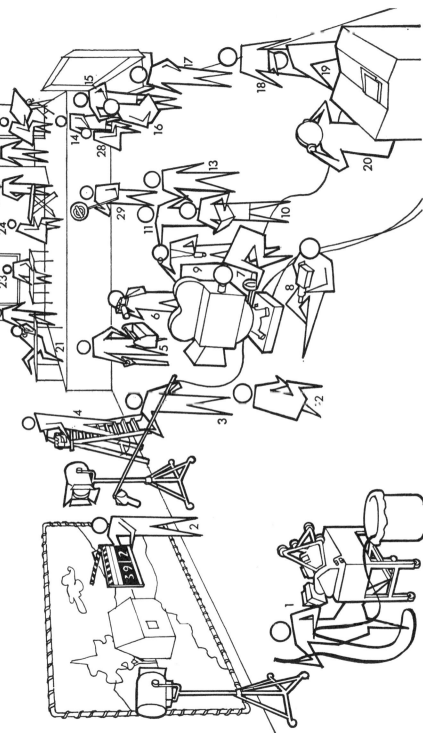

Anatomy of a film production: 1, Editor; 2, Clapper/Loader; 3, Assistant sound engineer (Boom operator or boom swinger); 4, Painter; 5, Unit carpenter; 6, Stills photographer; 7, Camera operator; 8, Producer/director; 9, Director of photography; 10, Continuity girl; 11, First assistant director; 12, Assistant cameraman (Focus puller); 13, Associate producer; 14, Chief make-up artist; 15, Hair stylist; 16, Actress; 17, Police liaison; 18, Rigger; 19, Electrician—one of perhaps a dozen working on the film; 20, Sound engineer; 21, Publicity director; 22, Production accountant; 23, Production manager; 24, Wardrobe supervisor; 25, Screenwriter; 26, Author; 27, Art director; 28, Actor; 29, Property master.

finds in the long run that he gets much more out of the unit if he keeps them all happy. Regardless of varying opinions expressed about the rushes, the director uses the take that *he* wants.

Working with the actor

It is sometimes difficult for a cameraman to provide a high standard of photography all the time without conflicting with the way in which the scene is played, the movement of the actors, and without causing any hold up in the production. But this is the way it has to be. He must fit his lighting to the scene as it stands.

Although he can prepare all his lighting on a rehearsal sequence, he relies on the actor to be consistent in his movements as well as his performance. If the actor varies his actions from those rehearsed he can move into poor lighting and spoil the whole scene. He could even pass right outside the limits of the set.

To serve as a guide for the actor, key marks are made on the floor and he must hit each of these positions at certain points in the take. This requires some sense of timing because he may have to move to several places in one take. He must repeat this performance and these movements each time the take is attempted, without becoming tired or stilted and always arriving at the same places at the correct times.

A well-known actor sometimes has a double who works as a stand-in. Normally, a stand-in is not photographed, but used for the rehearsals only. He serves as a "tailor's dummy" for lighting, focus and movements in rehearsals. But sometimes he may be so like the actor in figure and face that he can pass as his double in a long shot when wearing the same clothes or a similar suit to the actor. He may be a crowd man working also as a stand-in but occasionally he is something of a stunt man as well and will do things which might have injured the actor and so held up the production.

Viewing rushes, a daily routine

Film of the day's work is processed overnight at the laboratory and proof prints are quickly made in time to be viewed by the production team the following morning. These prints are called rushes or dailies, because viewing rushes is a daily routine. Generally there is a small projection theatre for this purpose at the studio.

Not all the day's work is printed. Some takes are known to be failures and are discarded. The director orders rush prints to be made only of those taken that are likely to be up to standard. There may be several takes that he wishes to see in the viewing theatre before making his selection. He may even find that no one take is exactly right all through but that he can use half of one take and half of another, perhaps with some close-ups in between as cutaways.

The takes viewed in the theatre are never regarded as trial runs. They are the actual material that will be used. Only in exceptional cases would the same shot be tried again after viewing the rushes. If there is uncertainty about a take, a second or third one is done at the time of shooting. This may take only twenty minutes. If the set-up is shot again the next day because the rushes proved inadequate, preparation of the shot takes very much longer. Lighting position, re-rehearsal of actors, camera position and many other things have to be assembled from scratch.

The viewing of rushes concerns the cameraman too, even though the director's verdict on any scene is final. Naturally the cameraman pays particular attention to the aspects that directly concern him, such as details of lighting, camera movement and composition, as well as focus and exposure. For the director the first consideration is usually the actor's performance but he too is influenced by the quality of a particular shot.

The cameraman, who here acts in an advisory capacity, is free to point out anything arising from his work and the director is usually glad of comment from an experienced cameraman. The cameraman can learn from viewing the rushes just how effective is any particular technique he has used in shooting the scene. Although he can tell at the time of shooting if a take is a certain failure, the finer points of the shot can only be judged accurately when the prints are seen.

The team in action

The director, cameraman and the operator work together from the beginning of each rehearsal. The actual take is in the sole charge of the operator, who uses the camera according to a plan worked out and agreed between the other two. All three look through the camera at one time or another and the operator pans and tilts the camera while the focus puller focuses, also according to plan.

The cameraman uses a director's viewfinder to frame up the scene. This enables him to see it just as it will appear on the film framed to similar proportions. He carries the viewfinder on a chain around his neck and uses it to look at preliminary set-ups before bringing in the camera. A Panavision finder has four lenses, wide angle, medium and long focus, which can be quickly changed from one to the other. These correspond in focal length with lenses fitted to the camera. The director usually has a similar viewfinder.

To guide the operator in the movement of the camera chalk marks are made on the floor. For a tracking shot chalk marks are made along the track where the camera must pause or change direction of movement. These marks indicate clearly the first, second and third time the camera must move or change direction.

The focus puller finds all his measurements with a tape measure.

He notes these on a sheet which he then tapes onto the camera. From this he can read off all the different focus points over the whole movement as it is rehearsed.

The operator is constantly looking through the camera as the director and the cameraman take turns to look through the other eyepiece. The design of the camera allows one person to look through the camera itself, while the other looks through the viewfinder at the side. The operator can follow their respective comments during the rehearsal and as he views the subject through the camera with each of them.

Meanwhile the sound man takes the opportunity of setting up his microphone and adjusting its position. Microphones must be in the most favourable spot for picking up the sound although they must not, of course, appear in the field of view of the camera. This must be specially guarded against if the camera is to be moved during the shot. The microphone may have to be shifted during the take and this movement too must be rehearsed. The sound man might have two or three microphones, either moving or hidden and listens all the time to the sound. Usually there are at least three men working on the sound equipment. One, wearing earphones, listens to and mixes the sound. Another moves the microphone and the third works the film machine that records the track.

Occasionally snow, wind and rain effects will also be included in the shot, and separate teams of people control these machines as and when required.

Everyone must rehearse to the satisfaction of everyone else, making sure that the effect of one piece of equipment does not interfere with that of another. In some shots the possible combinations of cross-interference are quite remarkable. The wind machine might blow onto a mike making a loud noise. So the wind has to be deflected from the mike. The snow might appear too thick in the foreground or be falling unevenly. Corrections and re-rehearsals have to be carried out constantly. When all preparations have been made and the final rehearsal completed, the first shot is attempted.

Second unit

A director might decide on a good location for a particular scene and use some of the interesting local characters or amenities. But on a big film, he cannot bite into his schedule by deviating from it to shoot some random material that happened to be attractive. If he wants a montage of scenic views without the actors he will probably send the second cameraman off for a day or two or perhaps a week to some remote area to get these shots. If on the other hand it involved a background for actors the whole thing would have to be planned. All actors parts are normally covered by the first unit. The planning and schedule procedure of a feature film are quite different from those of a documentary production where, if necessary, the crew can run around grabbing extra material off-the-cuff.

Second unit shots are sometimes taken under the instruction of the director but not with his personal supervision. A second unit director is often engaged, and he brings material back for the approval of the director. The first unit director having finished the main scenes with the actors and dialogue may leave the second unit director to round off with any long shots or sunset effects which may be necessary to complete the sequence.

In assembling the film the editor might suggest to the director that a certain shot would be very useful as a cutaway. If the director agrees, the second unit will be sent off to get it but normally the director is the originator of all shots made in the film. A film must be pretty strictly geared to the script throughout its production. Otherwise it would be impossible to schedule for costs and period of shooting.

2

Cameras and Lenses

THE CAMERAS USED in the feature film industry are often roughly categorized as studio and field types. The terms, however, are rather misleading as they imply that neither cameras are used in any environment but those by which they are entitled. This is not so.

BASIC CAMERA TYPES

The studio camera, a heavy instrument weighing perhaps a basic 50 lb without its magazines or other attachments, is nevertheless practically standard equipment for exterior work also in any situation where the camera can be mounted on a heavy duty support.

The field camera is usually a far lighter instrument which can be held in the hand or more normally supported by hands and shoulder, and operated in this fashion. Hand-held camera work is most commonly associated with documentary or television film usage where a certain degree of unsteadiness is acceptable owing to the relatively low ratio of enlargement required from the film frame to cover the television or small industrial screen. In feature film production, using 35-mm gauge film for example, such a lightweight camera would be used only where unsteadiness was consciously sought after as an effect, or it was quite impossible to use a mounted camera to gain accessibility or manoeuvrability in a particular scene. These cameras, though very suitable for exterior work, are by no means confined to it.

FILM SIZES AND SCREEN SYSTEMS

At this point it is necessary to distinguish between the various film sizes in use today and the screen *systems* based on these sizes. These systems determine the choice of camera and the particular lenses used with that camera.

A screen system, as such, is an established combination of certain mechanical and optical standards which are either unique to that system or shared with other established systems. Thus, 35-mm film, a universally adopted conventional film stock, is used in different systems to achieve widely differing end results.

In deciding any particular screen system the following factors must be determined. They are the variables of all widely used screen systems:

1 Gauge of the camera film stock
2 Relative dimensions of each picture frame on the camera stock
3 Optical systems used on the camera
4 Gauge of the film used to make the final projection print
5 Relative dimensions of picture frame on the print
6 Optical process used in printing the image.

Two gauges of film material are used as camera stock in the feature film industry today. These are 35 mm and 65 mm.*

The 35-mm gauge film has a long history, and dates back to the productions by Edison in 1890–91 but was not standardized until 1909. Today, it is still the most widely used, although the proportions of the actual picture frame on the film have been somewhat altered. The normal image proportion (aspect ratio) of straight 35-mm photography is 1·33:1 and the print made from this is similar. This is known as the Academy aperture.

However, several wide screen systems also use the 35-mm gauge and it is important to remember that the resultant screen proportions are the figures that matter rather than the camera apertures. So the cameraman should bear the final print aspect ratio in mind.

A popular wide-screen size is the 1·85:1 system using conventional camera optics and 35-mm film.

In the *Panavision 35* and *CinemaScope* systems, special anamorphic lenses are used on the camera to "squeeze" the horizontal image dimension into virtually the normal film frame size. From this camera negative either a squeezed image print is made, which is projected through an anamorphic lens giving a final screen image of 2·35:1, or it is unsqueezed when printed on special projection stock 70-mm wide giving a screen image aspect ratio of 2·2:1.

The *Techniscope* system uses no anamorphic lens on the camera, and gives a negative image with a two-perforation pulldown instead of the normal four-perforations per frame, i.e. a long, narrow (2·35:1 ratio) image. When the 35-mm projection print is made from this, the image is compressed into a squarer shape, which when projected through an

* Some feature films have been made on Super 16 mm, for subsequent printing onto 35 mm. It offers the possibility of hand held sync sound, but as much, if not more, attention must be paid to cleaning out the camera etc. as with 35 mm.

anamorphic lens is unsqueezed again to a screen image of 2·35:1. Though economical, there is inevitably some loss of screen definition with this system due to the smaller original negative area.

Still using 35-mm film, but with the frames positioned side by side along the film (which travelled horizontally in the camera) was the old *VistaVision* system. A print with reduced image size was made from this and when projected gave a 1·85:1 aspect ratio screen image.

The *Technirama* and *Super Technirama 70* systems used a similar horizontal frame placement, but a compressed image. In the case of Technirama the image was printed on 35-mm stock in a reduced form, but still compressed, which when projected gave a screen image of 2·35:1 aspect ratio. With *Super Technirama 70* the same camera negative was printed with a decompressed image onto 70-mm projection stock, which was projected through a normal lens giving a 2·21:1 aspect ratio screen image.

Not long after the introduction of wide-screen photography it was felt necessary to find some way of improving the general quality of the screen image. Among the systems adopted was one which departed from the use of standard 35-mm film and adopted instead a special camera stock 65 mm wide which offered a far larger image size. This is the basis of the *Todd-AO* and *Super Panavision 70* processes. The camera uses lenses giving an image of natural (unsqueezed) proportions on a long narrow frame across the film which travels vertically in the camera in the normal way. This is printed onto 70-mm projection stock, and the screen image has an aspect ratio of 2·21:1. No anamorphic lens is involved at any stage.

A later system, *Ultra-Panavision 70*, uses an anamorphic lens on the camera to produce a squeezed image in the same frame dimensions as the system above, on 65-mm film. From this, a squeezed image print is made onto 70-mm printing stock. When projected through an anamorphic lens the screen image is 2·2:1.

A further wide-screen system, *Cinerama*, originally employed three synchronized cameras to cover a total viewing angle of approximately 145°. The prints made by this process were simultaneously projected by three interlocked projectors onto a deeply curved screen. Later improvements to this system dispense with the triple camera and triple projector arrangement and use instead a single 65-mm camera producing a compressed image which is optically printed onto 70-mm film and shown on a single projector, still, however, covering adequately the special deep curve *Cinerama* screen. Nowadays *Cinerama* is shot on *Ultra Panavision* equipment.

Although 65 mm is now less frequently used for camera work 70 mm is popular for presentation in large cinemas (usually in the form of a blow-up from 35 mm) as it allows the enormous heat from the projector lamp to be spread over a larger area of film and provides room for four stereo tracks.

TYPICAL CAMERA MODELS

Only a handful of camera models are in very general use in the world's film studios, but a large number of lesser-known types are still to be found in countries where the film industry does not have the financial resources for the very latest equipment. A film camera is an expensive item for a studio or equipment hire firm. It is generally built to very high mechanical standards and, therefore, has a long working life. To discard such equipment simply because a further model has been introduced with marginal improvements would be extravagant. If the older model functions properly and is not inconvenient to use or incapable of some necessary duty such as use with a particular sound system, then it is kept in service.

Development in professional equipment has for many years seemed to lag behind that of the amateur: actually it is a matter only of economics. Although new cameras are available, many studios continue with older equipment which is considered by some people to be obsolescent or even obsolete.

REFLEX STUDIO CAMERAS

First choice for crews or films studios who give a high priority to operational convenience is certain to be a camera which provides a continuous view through the taking lens while filming. Two main systems of reflex viewing are currently used in 35-mm cameras.

With the spinning mirror system the shutter provides a (slightly flickering) image by passing light into the viewfinder between each exposure on the film (see also page 49). The other system uses a stationary pellicle mirror in the light path behind the lens. The pellicle is a fine membrane with semi-reflecting and semi-transmitting properties. Its surface reflects a certain proportion of the light into the viewfinder while the remainder passes through the pellicle to the film. A number of non-reflex cameras have been converted for reflex viewing by inserting such a pellicle and reflex viewfinder. One disadvantage with this system is that any pellicle placed in front of the film must result in some loss of transmission. In the Mitchell BNC SPR (Silent Pellicle Reflex) the resultant light loss is about $\frac{1}{4}$–$\frac{1}{3}$ of a stop. The viewing image, however, does not flicker.

The Mitchell BNCR reflex camera is an improved version of the BNC model (see below) using a stainless steel spinning mirror shutter (separate from the normal camera shutter though synchronized with it)

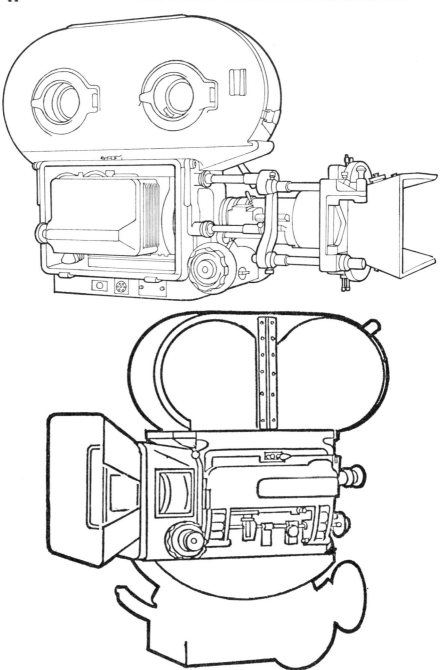

Reflex studio cameras: Panavision PSVR (*top*) has a 175° spinning mirror shutter (R 200 version has a 200° shutter) interchangeable with a pellicle mirror for use in front or rear projection work. The Panaspeed motor has fixed (24 and 25 fps) speeds and a continuous (8–32 fps) range. Mitchell BNC SPR (Silent Pellicle Reflex) (*bottom*), a version of the BNC modified for reflex viewing with a continuous image via a pellicle mirror.

which reflects a bright image into the viewfinder, where it is subsequently magnified. Apart from a reduction in camera noise level, additional
facilities at the front of the camera and of course the elimination of the
rack-over mechanism, the camera is generally similar to the BNC.

The Panavision Silent Reflex (PVSR) is a camera of recent design,
but is more compact and lighter in weight than the equivalent older
studio cameras. It has a dual register pin movement and double claws
for pull-down on four perforations. It uses a spinning mirror shutter
which may, if required, be interchanged with a pellicle for use in front
or back projection work, where continuous viewing is called for. This
camera has a 175° maximum shutter opening. The viewfinder image has
zoom magnification for convenience in focusing and, where necessary,
the image can be instantly de-anamorphosed. An alternative external
viewfinder is available for certain types of shot involving difficult or
rapid camera movement. Its auto-parallax correction can be disen-
gaged.

The mattebox on the camera allows a full complement of filters,
etc., and either 400- or 1000-ft film magazines may be mounted. There
is a standard 1000-ft magazine blimp.

The Panavision R 200 camera is a version with a 200° shutter. It
takes anamorphic or spherical lenses and a T/V viewfinder door. The
motor is variable for any running speed between 8 and 32 fps (a visible
tachometer is provided) and may be switched to crystal speed control
for 24 or 25 fps sync shooting.

RACKOVER STUDIO CAMERAS

A camera which has been held in great regard for several decades
is the Mitchell NC (or BNC) model. This has the rackover system for
viewfinding and focus, and shooting—a system which has in some
cameras been superseded by the reflex principle. With the rackover
mechanism the body of the camera containing the film drive, motor and
controls is shifted sideways by the operation of a lever. This brings a
focusing tube into position behind the lens affording an uninterrupted
view through it. The lens can be visually focused through the tube,
prior to taking the shot. The body is then racked back, shifting the
tube sideways and bringing the film aperture into position behind the
lens. Prior to this racking movement the focusing tube can serve as a
viewfinder and a second monitor finder can be used simultaneously.
When racked over ready for the take only the monitor finder is opera-
tive. Although it does not provide a view through the actual taking lens
it gives an accurate framing of the subject. Parallax error, resulting
from the slight displacement of the viewfinder to one side of the lens,
is automatically compensated for in the BNC camera. Viewfinders

are usually fitted with adjustable correction lenses to compensate for errors in the cameraman's eyesight.

The rackover system is common to Mitchell 35-mm and 65/70-mm (BFC) studio cameras and non-reflex studio cameras hired to producers by Panavision Inc., specialists in wide-screen cinematography systems.

The rackover system is, in fact, gradually being discarded in favour of the more convenient reflex method.

Lenses

The Mitchell NC model is fitted with a four-mount turret lens. This panel with four lenses may be revolved to position any one lens at the shutter aperture. Turning the panel gives a very quick interchange. With the BNC model, which has only one lens mount, the lens must be detached and replaced by another if a different focal length is needed. Alternatively a zoom lens can be fitted and the focal length selected on that.

Footage marks for setting focus, and aperture stops are engraved around each lens barrel and in the case of zoom lenses sometimes depth of field marks are included.

Mattebox and sunshade

Sliding on two parallel rods beneath the lens are a mattebox and sunshade. These are positioned immediately in front of the taking lens and may be adjusted to any position along the rods, then locked. The mattebox accommodates several kinds of accessory for special effects work in the camera. A rotating disc to take filters is also fitted. Image masking is possible on all four sides of the image by use of special mattes.

Shutter

The shutter is of the variable-opening type. By adjusting a knob and scale at the rear of the camera the shutter opening may be varied between an angle of 175° and zero. A rotating disc inside the shutter cuts the light off while the film is moving, but a segment in this disc allows the light through at the moment the film is arrested (twenty-four times a second at normal filming speed) for each exposure. The higher the running speed, generally, the greater the opening required in order to give the film sufficient exposure. On cameras such as the Mitchell, however, the size of the opening in the disc may be independently adjusted—an additional means of control over the exposure received by the film. The size of the opening is the "angle" or size of the segment in the disc. In the BNC model the shutter opening has an automatic dissolving control which produces fades (in or out) at the touch of a button.

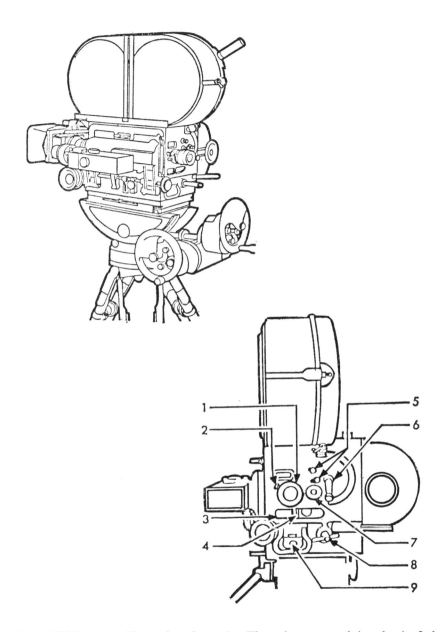

Mitchell BNC camera with soundproof magazine. The rackover system brings the viewfinder tube into position behind the taking lens, and is then returned to the normal position before shooting. Most of the controls are positioned on the back of the camera. Those shown are: 1, focusing eyepiece; 2, telescope magnification lever; 3, footage counter; 4, frame counter; 5, automatic dissolve controls; 6, hand dissolve lever; 7, miniature shutter; 8, rackover handle; 9, spirit level.

Motors

As with many cameras, motors on the Mitchell camera are externally mounted, and may be quickly detached and interchanged with others: leads from the power supply which plug into the motor can be transferred speedily to a new motor.

The motor drives the film through the camera, turning the shutter and the intermittent mechanism which pulls down each frame of film and arrests it for the moment of exposure. This type of motor is distinct from other external motors such as those used on some cameras to power the film magazine.

Five main types of camera motor are used: variable speed, interlocked, synchronous, crystal controlled and multi-duty.

The variable speed motor is used where no sound recording is made. It provides a wide range of filming speeds ranging from only a few frames per second to something in the region of double the standard filming speed. It is usually a rather noisy motor, but this does not matter, because sound recordings are rarely made in scenes where the camera is running at more or less than normal speed. A dial on the motor indicates the running speed.

The interlocked motor is soundproofed for use with synchronized sound shooting. It runs at a constant speed and can be locked to run precisely in step with another motor powering a sound recorder or in the case of slates for special backgrounds, with the special projector.

The synchronous motor can run at a constant speed for shooting with synchronous sound where a 50- or 60-cycle alternating current is available to act as a pacemaking control.

The crystal-controlled motor uses transistorized circuitry to amplify the frequency of a special quartz-type crystal which acts as a pulse to control rotation. A similar crystal motor on other cameras and the sound recorder will perfectly synchronize their speed without the need for connecting cables or common power supply

The multi-duty motor consists of two motors (220v AC 3-phase and 96v DC) on a common shaft. When current is applied to the DC motor it is speed-controlled by taking AC generated by the other motor, reading the frequency on a counter, and then setting the DC supply so that the speed is correct.

A special 25 fps motor is also available for filming T/V screens.

Magazines

Film is contained in a separate magazine which is first loaded in a darkroom or changing bag and then fitted onto the camera. The end of the spool of unexposed film is threaded through a light trap in the magazine, forms an external loop and then passes through another light trap back into the magazine and onto a take-up spindle. The magazine, completely light-tight when closed, is mounted on the camera and the film loop threaded through the camera mechanism. Several such magazines are kept ready and loaded and can be quickly interchanged in daylight.

Drive to the magazine is provided by a belt and drive-wheel transmitting power to the magazine from the main camera motor.

Controls

The main controls on the Mitchell NC camera are the film footage and frame counters, the shutter control and shutter opening indicator, inching wheel for turning the motor by hand, the starting switch and the adjustable eyepiece focusing tube. The BNC model has, in addition, controls for producing a dissolve automatically on the camera and a remote control focusing facility. These controls are positioned at the back of the camera.

Footage counters are provided for both magazine and camera, with another control permitting them to be re-set to zero when required. A frame counter is provided for use when absolute frame reckonings are necessary.

REFLEX FIELD CAMERAS

A typical lightweight camera of this description is the Arriflex 35 11C. Its considerably smaller size and lighter weight compared with a studio camera, makes a camera of this type suitable for mobile use, hand-held photography where needed and placement in constricted areas where a large studio camera could not be used. The camera is designed to be held in the hand but can equally well be mounted on a tripod. A special sound blimp makes it suitable for use in the studio, although a model of the Arriflex is self-blimped as indeed are some other cameras of the type. The self-contained blimp adds considerably to the weight, although the camera may still be held in the hand when necessary.

Reflex viewfinder

The most distinguishing feature of the Arriflex is the reflex viewfinder which, by using a mirror shutter positioned in the light path at 45° to the film plane, throws an intermittent image into the viewfinder. Thus the scene is viewed in a series of rapidly flickering images seen *between* each exposure of the film. The sole disadvantage of this system is that at the end of a take the shutter may come to rest at the "open" position, i.e. where light passes through to the film and no image is

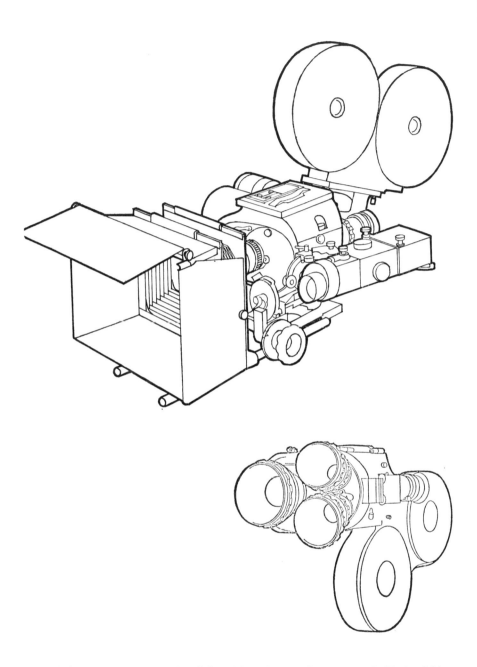

The Mitchell S35R Mk. 2. This is a lightweight noiseless reflex camera suitable for field or studio use, and may be blimped for sound stage work. It is shown here (*top*) with accessories such as mattebox and 1000-ft film magazine, and (*below*) with 400-ft magazine mounted below which rests on the shoulder when the camera is hand held in the field. This view also shows the divergent-mounted tri-lens turret.

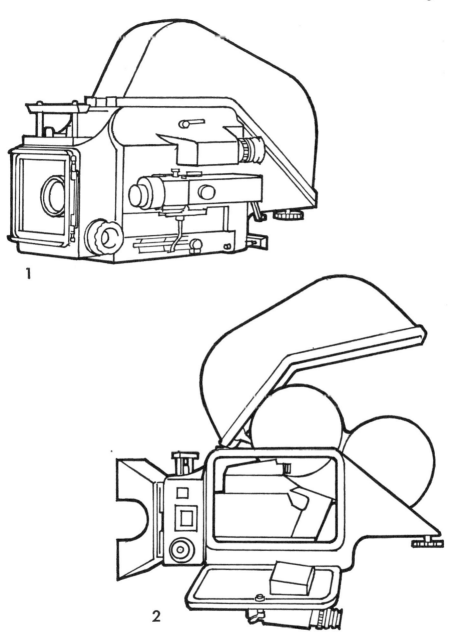

Blimpted multi-purpose reflex camera, Mitchell S35R Mk. 2, fitted with a lightweight sound blimp 1, allowing reflex viewing and the use of an external follow-focus Mitchell viewfinder. There are external controls for focusing, viewfinder magnification, motor inching and the insertion of contrast viewing filters. The blimp has a filter holder and lenshood clamp, and basher lamps may be clamped directly onto it. It is shown 2, with the side hatch and camera open for access to the film path, gate, etc., and opened at the top to allow magazines to be interchanged.

visible in the viewfinder. The shutter can be turned manually with a small inching knob to correct this.

The main benefit of this system is that the subject can be viewed throughout the take when looking through the camera in exactly the form it will take on the film. The effect of the selected depth of field can be seen and framing is always correct without the alignment of a monitor viewfinder or any form of parallax compensation due to the different location of viewing and taking lens. No preparatory rackover is necessary.

Since the introduction of this type of camera in 1938 a number of other makes have appeared using the same reflex viewing principle.

Other features

The Arriflex has a high quality intermittent mechanism with a steadying device which acts upon each frame at the moment of exposure. Drive to the magazine (400-ft or 1000-ft load) is via a direct mechanical link engaged when the magazine is attached. The magazine is in other respects similar to those used on studio cameras. It has a built-in footage counter.

Other facilities are a variable-opening shutter, adjustable sunshade and mattebox, on/off switch, filming speed indicator, adjustable-focus eyepiece with a special viewfinder shutter which opens when the eye is pressed against it but otherwise remains closed to prevent light from reaching the film via the reflex viewing system. The viewfinder gives a magnified image.

The motor for the Arriflex is cylindrical in shape and is attached beneath the body and perpendicular to it, forming a natural grip for hand-held camera work. Variable speed motors are available, one of which is designed specifically to run at greater than normal filming speed. A synchronous motor with built-in footage counter is made for sync sound shooting. Constant speed motors can also be obtained for this camera.

The Mitchell S35R Mk. 2 is a lightweight noiseless multi-purpose reflex camera with an intermittent movement similar to that of the Mitchell BNC (dual pull-down claws engaging four perforations, and dual register pins) and uses a separate spinning mirror shutter with blades at 45° to the film for reflex viewfinding. The variable film shutter has a maximum opening of 170°. The camera is adaptable for studio work by attaching accessories, and can be blimped for use on a sound stage. A 400-ft magazine is mounted beneath the camera for shoulder holding and field work but the camera will also take 1000-ft Mitchell magazines which are mounted on the top. Other facilities or accessories include: interchangeable motors, sunshade and filter slots, separate parallax-corrected monitor viewfinder, T/V monitor system, powered

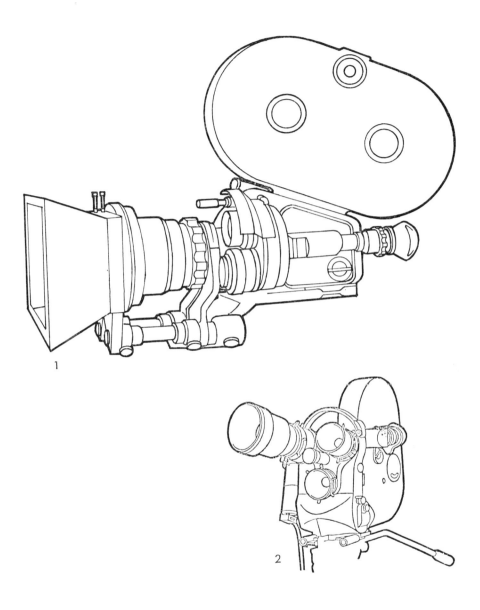

Reflex field cameras. 1, Arriflex 35, a spinning mirror reflex camera which may be hand held, shown here with a 400-ft magazine and zoom lens with hood (sunshade) which needs extra support to avoid strain on the lens mount. 2, Eclair Cameflex CM3 camera with three-lens turret and self-contained magazine. A very versatile design that allows rapid interchange of magazines.

zoom control, follow-focus attachment, a matte-matching device for use while shooting and an underwater housing.

A multi-purpose lightweight camera used in France and some other countries is the Eclair Cameflex. It has a reflex mirror shutter viewing system, 200° shutter and a film magazine with self-contained drive mechanism, allowing the magazines to be changed very rapidly.

CAMERA SUPPORTS

Some form of steady and level support is essential for the motion picture camera. By far the majority of shots are taken from a solid mechanical base of one kind or another. Only a very few are hand-held in feature film production and many cameras are in any case far too heavy for such techniques.

Tripod

The basic camera support is the tripod. This is usually either made from tubular stainless steel, or, in the case of older models, is of wooden construction with metal fittings. Spiked tips to each leg prevent the legs from spreading with the outward thrust due to the weight of the camera mounted on it. A tripod of the type in wide use today provides a lens height of between 4 and 5 ft when the legs are in the normal position and between 7 and 8 ft when the outer sections of each leg are extended to full height. The height varies slightly according to the spread of the legs, the camera in use and the type of head fitted to the tripod.

Tripod heads

Tripod heads are designed to provide for two basic camera movements, panning and tilting. The pan/tilt head allows almost any degree of adjustment in these horizontal and vertical planes. With the pan action on any tripod head, the camera may be revolved through a complete circle. The tilt is restricted to less than a semicircle. The camera cannot usually be tilted beyond or perhaps even near to the vertical upward or downward position. On all heads the camera may be positioned and then locked in either one or both planes.

Geared head

This head, of heavy duty construction and suitable for studio use, provides adjustment by handwheels in either plane. These wheels are geared so that a gradual and smooth adjustment of camera is possible. This is desirable for movements made during the take. More rapid movements must be made with a rapid gear (fitted to two-speed models)

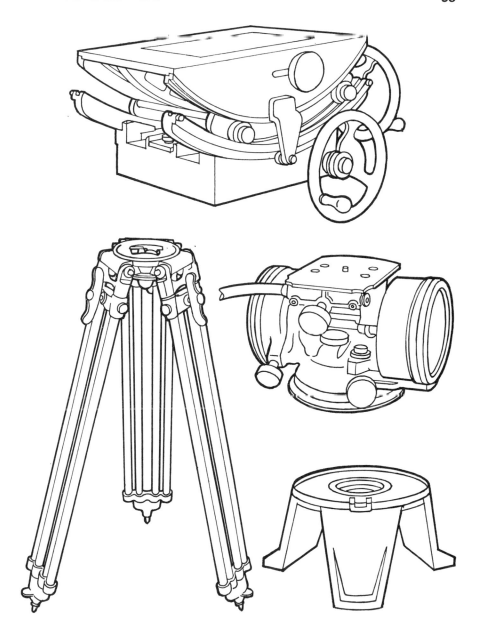

Standard geared pan and tilt head (*top*) mounted on top of tripod (*left*) which may be made of wood but is more often of tubular steel construction. A fluid head (*centre right*) smooths camera movement by operating against the resistance of fluid forced through a small aperture from one compartment to another. A high hat (*bottom*) is a small mount of fixed height on which the camera stands when operating from low level or elsewhere when a few inches of extra height is needed.

or the pan/tilt handle fitted as an option on others. In this case the head can move freely and does not require geared adjustment.

Friction head

This works on the principle that a moderate resistance offered to the action of panning or tilting the camera irons out any unevenness in these actions. In practice this provides a simple and very smooth movement at any speed and is frequently used for location shooting owing to its lighter general construction than the geared type.

Fluid and gyro heads

Fluid heads use enclosed chambers of fluid in place of the mechanical resistance of the grease-loaded friction head. They are available in light- and medium-weight models, the medium-weight model being suitable to take the Mitchell BNC or a camera of equivalent size. One model has, as an additional extra, a special bowl fitting with which the camera can be quickly levelled without any adjustment of the tripod legs.

Gyro heads use a geared flywheel to provide smooth resistance to movement of the head. This is usually provided for pan movements only. The speed of movement (i.e. resistance) on some models is adjustable.

Stabilizers

Gyro stabilizers can steady a hand-held 35-mm camera used from a vibrating platform when the vibrations are not wanted in the shot. Such a stabilizer is an advantage when filming from a car, or improvised dolly for example, as well as for any air or sea photography where movement must be minimized, though they are in less frequent use nowadays than the Dynalens or Tyler helicopter mount.

The stabilizer attaches to the base of the camera and works on the gyroscopic principle. Power is supplied by two batteries (giving about three hours operating duration unless the recharger is used) and the total weight of the stabilizer itself is approximately 3 lb. The less weight placed on the stabilizer the more effective is its performance. Cameras should use the smaller type of film magazine if possible.

Another form of stabilizer provides a steady surface for cameras weighing up to 60 lb (or with a special attachment 150-lb camera) operating from a flat surface. The stabilizer can be bolted down and the legs of the tripod attached to three brackets.

A counterweight system adjusts the camera weight and a control lever is provided to adjust the tension of stabilization.

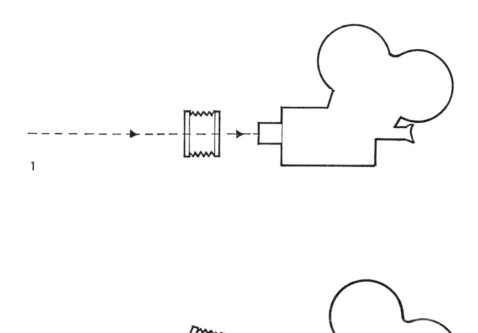

Dynalens. A device for stabilizing the image when the camera is subjected to vibration. A variable refraction element is mounted in front of the camera lens. The element is a fluid compartment contained within movable glass plates. The vibrations are transmitted through a servo control to operate the glass plates vertically or horizontally and produce a defection of the image to cancel out the effect of the movement.

Dynalens system

The Dynalens is an optical camera-steadying device which also employs gyro stabilization. It is actually a lens with dynamic properties consisting of a liquid-filled compartment enclosed by two movable glass sheets, and is fitted in front of the camera lens.

Any movement of the glass sheets shifts the image on the film, because with the liquid-filled space between them the sheets form an adjustable optical wedge. The lens uses a system of gyroscopic stabilizers to provide a mean steadiness. Any sudden camera movement exercised against these, sets off a control mechanism to shift the lens. The gyroscopic sensing systems respond to the vibration and this is transmitted via servo amplifiers to the glass sheets. As a result, the film image is instantaneously shifted in the opposite direction by an amount equal to the shift that would have been caused by the sudden camera movement. The lens is designed to respond only to sudden movements, so that it does not interfere with normal camera pans.

All camera vibrating effects can be eliminated with this lens but when sudden pans and tilt movements are wanted without compensation, the lens can be made inoperative.

Hydraulic and manual elevators

An elevator is a versatile form of camera support column used instead of a tripod either directly on the floor or on a dolly. It is used in virtually every production.

It consists of a metal multi-section central column which carries the mounting plate for pan/tilt heads. Brackets from the foot of the column carry a seat and, on the opposite side, a counter-weight to compensate for any unbalance caused by the operator's weight. Both these items can be adjusted. The whole is mounted on a solid base plate which in turn is fixed to a low-angle bracket. The mounting plate at the top can be quickly levelled by adjustment of the three retaining screws and the whole upper section can be raised or lowered by applying or reducing hydraulic pressure from the pump at the base of the unit.

The manual elevator is another version which uses a hand wheel at the side to raise or lower the camera on the central column. Manual elevators have now largely been replaced by the hydraulic type.

Other camera supports

Various forms of support are available for use with lightweight 35-mm cameras. A camera support bracket is made which fits over the shoulder and leaves the cameraman's hands free to operate focus and zoom controls. The same freedom of action is possible with a camera harness which fits round the cameraman's body. Other forms of shoulder

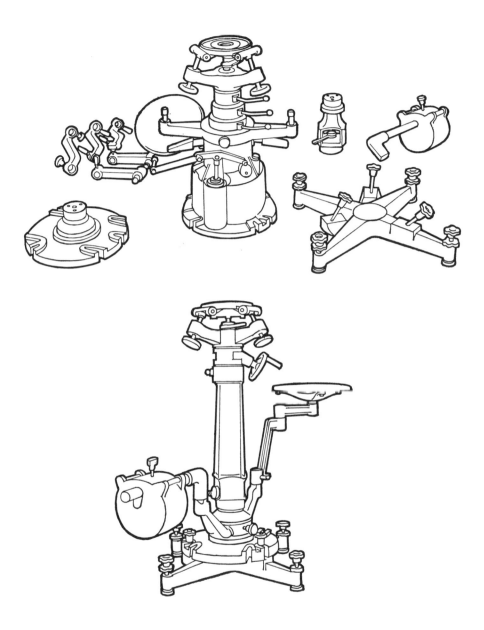

Hydroelevator (Elemack) and its accessories (*top*). The hydraulic camera column replaces the conventional tripod for many situations. The central section is extended hydraulically with a pump and each section may be adjusted individually. There is an operator's seat and counterweight and the column may be used free standing or mounted on a dolly. The earlier manually operated version (*below*) showing seat and counterweight in position, is raised and lowered by a hand wheel. Both columns have a quick-acting camera leveller at the top which has a Mitchell fitting to accept geared heads.

pod, pistol grip or sling are manufactured for use with specific camera models.

Camera rostrums are made in lightweight metal sections providing a choice of several operating heights up to about 6 ft.

The hi-hat is a specially made support for the camera which is used near floor level. It is about 8 in. high and a tripod head can be fitted to the top to give pan and tilt movements. The hi-hat can be attached to the floor or platform when required. It can sometimes be fitted to a tripod to give the camera an extra few inches of height.

The wedge is a device for fitting btween the tripod head and the camera to give a greater angle of tilt than is possible with the head alone. A wedge may be designed to give a fixed elevation of 25° or 35° or it may be adjustable for any angle up to 90°. Models are available for use with "wild" or blimped cameras.

A rolling tripod spider is a wheeled assembly that fits underneath a tripod, allowing it freedom of movement over flat surfaces, and is also used for tracking or crabbing during the shot. Wheels on the spider can be locked for any movement straight or crabwise. Heavy duty or lightweight models are available for use with the two basic forms of camera equipment. Some rolling spiders have a control to raise or lower the effective height of the camera.

TRAVELLING CAMERA SUPPORTS

Tracking is one of the most frequently used camera movements, and mobile camera mountings are made to provide this movement under varying conditions. The basic problem with any tracking movement is to keep the camera steady enough during the shot so that slow movements are imperceptible and rapid movements contain the minimum vibration. An absolutely flat surface is the ideal for tracking, but the surface as well as being *even* must also be level. In such conditions (i.e. in the studio) the camera can be mounted on a simple dolly with pneumatic rubber tyres, which will provide sufficient smoothness. On rougher surfaces which are still level it may be necessary to lay down special tracks and mount the camera on a dolly fitted with suitable wheels. Unlevel surfaces may either have to be properly levelled out before the tracks go down or if it is not too serious, the tracks may be levelled out by applying packing material or wedges beneath them at certain points. The horizon line seen in the camera viewfinder must not develop a slant nor should it suddenly move up or down simply because the camera is not level. On certain locations, such as in the desert, the sand can be bulldozed flat, then watered down and rollered well enough to give a hard level surface for non-tracked camera supports.

Dolly

This, apart from the rolling spider, is the smallest form of mobile support. In some studios it is known as a trolley, or truck. It is basically a low platform mounted on four wheels with a push bar and a wheel-locking device at one end. In the centre is a camera mounting, perhaps with a hi-hat on top. The conventional pan and tilt head is fitted above this with the camera resting on its top plate. A single seat for the operator is placed on a bracket fastened to the central support in some way. In place of the simple mounting with hi-hat, there may be a hydraulic elevator.

On some models the central column unit can be moved into various positions for convenience. Alternatively the conventional tripod can be used and fixing points are provided to secure the feet.

Some dollys run on pneumatic rubber tyres which can be steered by a driving wheel located next to the push bar. When the dolly is needed for straight-line tracking the wheels may be locked off parallel.

A dolly with rubber tyres can be run in metal channel tracks. In this case solid rubber tyres may be used, but in the US low-pressure pneumatic-tyred dollys are often run in wood channel tracks. Solid rubber is satisfactory for tracking on good existing surfaces or where plyboards have been laid beforehand.

Tubular steel rails can be supplied for straight or curved tracking. The dolly wheels are replaced by grooved bogey wheels which work on a similar basis to lengthy units of railway stock. Curves of two radii are produced and the straight sections are made in several standard lengths. When dollys are adapted to run on tracks the steering becomes inoperative and the wheel is removed.

This type of dolly with or without tracks can take the heaviest blimped cameras plus the cameraman and the focus puller.

A smaller but more elaborate form of camera dolly can be steered by two wheels or by all four. It is fitted with pneumatic tyres and has the same load capacity. Four-wheel steering allows crab movements, i.e. all the wheels are locked off at an angle to the dolly frame but parallel with one another. The dolly can then move obliquely relative to the subject rather like a crab. Tyres can be interchanged with solid rubber, or bogies for tubular tracking.

A special type of dolly is manufactured for use in very confined spaces. This corridor dolly has a width only half that of conventional dollys (i.e. 20 in.). Fitted with bogey wheels for tubular tracks the dolly accepts hydraulic or manual camera columns or a tripod.

A dolly of most unusual configuration is the Elemack Octopus which has hinged wheels that can be arranged in any of twelve positions

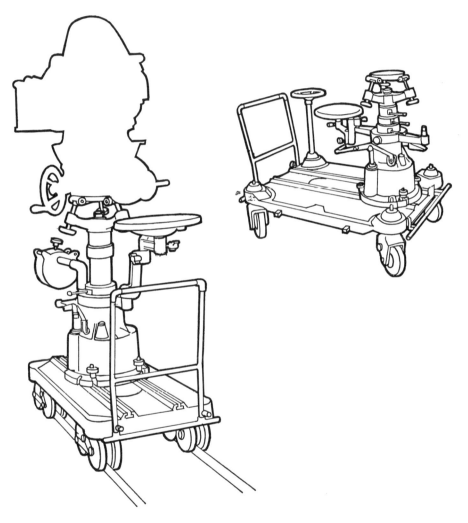

Small dollys. Elemack hydroelevator camera column mounted on a corridor dolly (*left*), a very narrow dolly for tracking in restricted space such as the corridor of a railway carriage. The bogey wheels run on tubular steel tracks which can be laid quite quickly. Elemack camera column on a small platform dolly (*right*) which can be steered by two, or all four wheels for crab shots or locked for running in a straight line. This dolly is small enough to pass through normal doorways.

so that it can be used in cramped conditions or small ill-shaped operating areas. It can crab and be locked for straight tracking or steered by two wheels only for curved tracking. It can be adapted for use on tubular straight or curved track and needs an operating area no wider than a corridor dolly. Both types are suitable for tracking through narrow doors, railway corridors, etc.

Location dollys

The mobile camera support for location work often needs to be of more substantial construction than its studio equivalent. Some such location equipment can be of enormous proportions compared with studio facilities.

The Oxberry Continental hydraulic dolly is therefore considered a lightweight unit although it weighs more than twice as much as the standard type of dolly described above. This dolly is fitted with a hydraulic jib (with seat) to provide vertical movements giving a lens height adjustable from 2 ft 3 in. to 6 ft 6 in. The dolly can be steered on its pneumatic tyres, or a change to solid tyres is made so that it can be run on aluminium flanged tracks. There are large frontal and side platforms and the dolly is propelled by means of the usual push bar at the back.

Crab dolly

The Moviola crab dolly is a typical representative of a most versatile form of dolly. The camera is positioned on a boom operated by hydraulic pressure. The boom is on a trolley with stepped bodywork providing working or access platforms of various levels. Seats are provided for camera operator and focus puller on the boom and main structure. The dolly runs on four pneumatic double-tyre wheels. The steering is operated by a control bar at the rear and wheels can be turned through a full circle so that oblique, right angle, curved or rotating movements can be achieved without difficulty. The maximum elevation possible with this dolly is 5 ft 9 in. (with ancilliary hi-hat) and the minimum 1 ft 10 in. The camera mounting on the boom is self-levelling and compensates for all changes of boom angle. This dolly weighs about half as much again as the location dolly mentioned above. It is essentially a flat-surface running vehicle and is not designed for use on metal or wood tracks. It has been very widely adopted for studio purposes.

Velocilator

Another form of dolly is the Edmonton Velocilator. This works on somewhat similar lines to those above but is very much heavier, weighing about 10 cwt. One important difference, however, is that the camera boom as well as moving vertically can rotate horizontally, allowing greater mobility for camera positioning.

Mini crane

A special lightweight crane is manufactured which can be fitted to a crab dolly or similar tracking vehicle. It is primarily intended for location use in areas of limited movement. The crane is pivoted on a central support with counterweight on the other end of the boom. A parallelogram arm maintains a level position for the camera platform and mounting where the operator sits.

Crane (Boom)

A still larger camera support is the crane, or boom, as it is known in the US. This, in its standard size, is much heavier than a Moviola crab dolly but provides an immense amount of scope for positioning the camera. The trolley section supports a central pillar which is the pivoting point of a very large parallelogram arm. At one end is the self-levelling camera platform fitted with the usual form of camera mounting and two or three seats according to the model—for its operator, focus puller and, on three-seat models, the director. At the other end is a counterweight.

Some cranes are operated manually, others by an electric or hydraulic power system. Manual operation is generally by an assistant who stands at the counterweight end of the boom moving it up or down as required and locking it in any position selected. For this purpose he often stands on a special platform at the back. On other models the boom movements are controlled from the camera platform as the operator requires. The boom can be raised, lowered or swivelled at will. On some models the central pillar may also be raised and lowered. The crane is often a tracked vehicle with bogies running on square-section track. The dolly pusher works from the off side when the camera is not in the way.

A larger form of crane is made in the US. This is the Chapman Titan. It has an immense powered boom which raises the camera and operators as high as 27 ft if necessary and is mounted on a large six-wheeled track body with pneumatic tyres. This is a self-powered crane and could be considered a distant relative of the television camera dolly. It can be used for outdoor speed sequences with fast tracking as it can be driven at speeds up to about 55 mph. Equipment of this scale, weighing up to 10 tons, is used only on large-scale productions.

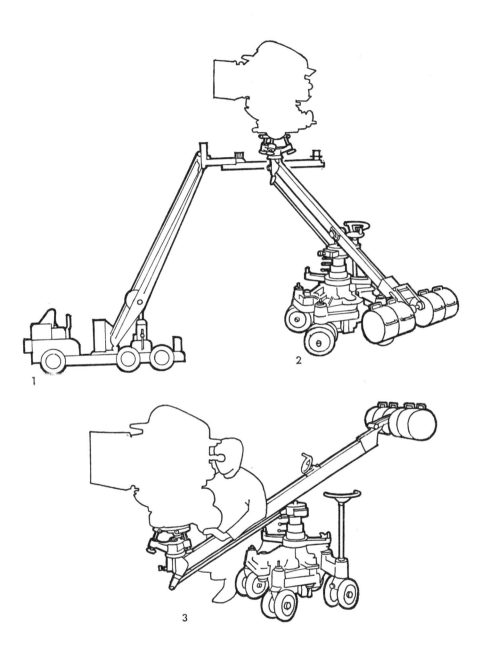

Camera cranes, or booms: 1, the Chapman Titan, a very large crane for location work, built on a heavy six-wheel truck base. 2 and 3, an Elemack crane with self-levelling platform and fitted with counterweights to take a heavy, blimped camera. It is based on the Elemack hydro-elevator and dolly with double tyres

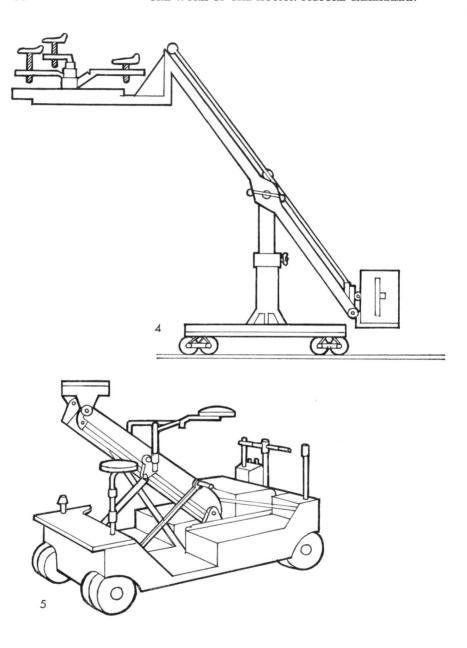

4, A large crane designed to run on rails. The three-seat platform remains in a horizontal position because of the parallelogram arm construction and is counterbalanced by weights at the opposite end. 5, Moviola Crab-Dolly. Fitted with pneumatic tyres. This well-equipped dolly allows smooth movement diagonally, around curves and in fact in almost any direction. The jib is raised and lowered hydraulically from a reservoir fitted with an electric pump, and operates quietly. There is a seat for the operator and focus puller, and side and end platforms may be fitted. Steering and hydraulic controls are at the rear.

Lens mounting

Two forms of lens mount are currently in wide use, single mount and turret mount. A single mount takes one lens only and a camera with this fitting is simpler to manufacture (and consequently lower priced) and lighter in weight. Where these factors matter, it is obviously better to take advantage of them. A single-mount camera is not very quick to operate, however, because for each change of focal length the lens must be removed and then replaced by another. But this drawback is not apparent if a zoom lens is used, as all focal lengths can be selected at will merely by operating the zoom lever. Moreover, the single mount is usually a very rigid attachment point on the camera for a zoom lens which may be rather heavy and long. A lens turret may be rigid but some are not.

The lens turret is a rotating plate fitted to the front of the camera. Three or four lenses are ranged around the plate and by rotating it, any of these may be brought into the shooting position, i.e. directly over the camera aperture (gate). With several lenses crowded together in so small a space they would tend to appear in one another's fields of view. A wide-angle lens may include a part of the barrel of a long focus lens. Consequently, turrets are often designed to hold the lenses on divergent axes. Even so if lenses not designed for the camera are used this trouble can recur. It is therefore wise to check this beforehand, and if possible mount the offending lens in the socket farthest from the wide angle.

Lens types

Many cameras are provided with a wide range of lenses specially designed for use with those cameras. But a number of other firms produce lenses of different construction and focal length for use on various cameras.

It is not unusual to have a choice of six or seven different focal lengths, ranging from wide angle (say, 25 mm, giving about 50° angle of view) to standard focal length (i.e. corresponding to normal human vision) with 35-mm cameras. With such a range of image magnifications at his disposal the cameraman can tackle most situations. There are occasions, however, when for an even wider view, a lens such as the Cooke Series III $f2$, 18-mm or the Angenieux Retrofocus $f3.5$, 14.5-mm, or even the Kinoptik $f1.9$, 9.8-mm, a super-wide-angle lens giving a view of 108° on 35-mm cameras, might be brought in.

At the opposite end of the scale are such lenses as the Cooke Telepanchro $f2.8$, 152-mm, the Telestigma $f4.6$, 228-mm, the Dallmeyer $f5.6$, 300-mm, or the Kilfitt Sport-fern-Kilar $f5.6$, 600-mm or Birns and

Sawyer Omnitar $f4\cdot5$, 1000-mm lenses. These longer focal length lenses are intended for conditions where tremendous image magnification is needed, for example, with unaccessible subjects of small scale at a distance when there is no better way to obtain a large image. A number of manufacturers made lenses in a full range of focal lengths.

All lenses have focus adjustment and iris control for setting the *f*-number or T-number. The *f*-number is the effective diameter of the lens opening and therefore as a figure represents its light passing power. T-numbers are a more precise (or academic) way of arriving at the same means of control. The T stands for transmission and represents the total light-transmitting power of the lens, taking into account such factors as cause any light losses in the optical system. The *f*-stop is a purely mathematical relationship. Though T-stops are more accurate, the difference between T- and *f*-stops in practice is minute, unless you are working with lenses which contain many elements, such as zoom lenses. Nevertheless, T-stops are the system most generally adopted and, in fact, some lenses are marked only with them.

Zoom lenses

Zoom lenses are adjustable continuously through a range of magnifications, but they cover only the middle range of focal lengths. The range may extend, for example, from 25 mm to 250 mm. Extreme wide-angle and long focus lenses are considerably shorter and longer than these. The range is expressed as a ratio, in this case 10:1. An even more versatile lens may have a ratio of 20:1 giving a focal length range of 25 mm to 500 mm. On the few occasions when greater or less magnification is needed a fixed focal length lens can be mounted. Generally, the longer the range of focal lengths available on a zoom lens the smaller its maximum working aperture is likely to be. Typical aperture/focal range relationships on currently available lenses are T2·8 on a 20–100-mm, T3 on a 20–120-mm and T9 on a 25–500-mm lens.

Special practical advantages of the zoom lens are that the focal length can be adjusted to frame the subject perfectly without moving the camera, rapid changes are possible from one focal length to another between shots, and the zoom movement itself can be an optical effect.

Focusing is more positive if advantage is taken of the restricted depth of field afforded by a long focal length and wide aperture. The zoom lens is, therefore, usually focused at maximum focal length and aperture and the focal length is then reset according to shooting requirements. The modern zoom lens holds focus on any distance once it has been set, whereas earlier types had to be refocused when the focal length was changed. However, with all zoom lenses an exact flange focal depth is critical in order to hold focus throughout the zoom. If there is not a correct relationship between lens and film the lens would drift out of focus when zooming to wide-angle.

Two optical characteristics common to all long focus lenses are present in a zoom lens. As the lens is moved to a longer focal length setting the subject appears unnaturally forshortened, and the depth of field diminishes. So precise focus-pulling technique is called for with moving subjects at a distance when the shot is also zoomed. Unfortunately, it is rather easy to forget these points when working with a zoom lens, particularly if the early part of a shot is at a relatively short focal length.

Zoom lenses are very important in modern film making. However, they are occasionally used over enthusiastically by the inexperienced. It becomes quite monotonous when zooms appear frequently in a film. A much more subtle mode of use is to combine the zoom effect with tracking and panning. Zoom lenses powered by electric motors allow you the choice of several steady zoom speeds. A very slow zoom when combined with panning and tracking does not appear as a zoom at all. Properly executed, the audience may never notice a zoom shot in a film, even though the production team used one on every day of shooting.

Over a long shot which involves tracking you might follow the actors and end on a close shot so that the director can cover the whole scene without need of a cut. A zoom can take the place of a tracking shot if it is done in a certain way. A fast zoom can be used for shock effect.

This is a favourite device for television but the special circumstances of TV require a different technique.

65-mm lenses

The standard focal length for 65-mm wide-screen photography is about 85 mm (approx. 35° angle of view). There is not such a range of lenses available for this size, but a fully equipped camera unit could expect to have five focal lengths at their disposal. These, in the case of Panavision lenses, would include a 25-mm Auto Panatar, (ultra wide) 50-mm Panatar, 55-mm Macro Panatar (a lens with an exceptionally long focusing range, down to 10 in.). With the exception of the 55-mm, all these lenses have a minimum focusing distance of 4–5 ft without optical assistance, and could be used on a BNC or NC camera (see page 45). The 50-mm has an exceptionally large working aperture, $f1$. A set of lenses comparable to these would give a reasonable flexibility of operation with two lenses for special situations.

Zoom lenses for 65 mm do not have as great a range of focal length as those designed for use on 35-mm cameras. A ratio of 3:1 or 3·5:1 is generally the maximum. The minimum focus range (without attachment) is about 5 ft.

Zoom image quality

Despite great improvements in image quality from zoom lenses, until recently it still had to be admitted that no such lens, for 35-mm or 65-mm use at least, could give the critical performance of the best individual lens. Still, no zoom lens offers the wide aperture nor the extremes of focal length of conventional lenses. If an optic is added to a zoom lens to vary its performance, it must, inevitably, have some slightly detrimental effect on image quality. True this may not matter in some circumstances or certain scenes where absolute maximum sharpness is not so important. But practically every manufacturer who has marketed zoom lenses or optical accessories for them also markets a range of conventional lenses. It is claimed that the performance of the best zoom lenses of recent design is now almost indistinguishable from that of single focal length lenses.

Power controls for zoom lenses

A special motor control is available for use with zoom lenses. It is a small 12-V electric unit providing, at the touch of a switch, automatic zooming which is both smooth and constant in speed. On most power controls the zooming speed can be varied at will. A typical model with two speed ranges provides a zoom movement through the whole range of focal length of from 5 seconds to 60 seconds and with an alternative drive gear from $2\frac{1}{2}$ seconds to 12 seconds. The limits for any zoom shot can be selected beforehand by adjustment of two arresting devices fitted to the lens.

SPECIAL LENSES

Pack shot lenses

In a frequently used camera shot, a subject is seen at close range and then almost immediately the camera moves upward and there is a quick change of focus to another subject or scene in the middle or far distance. With an ordinary lens, supposing it could focus close enough in the first place, this shift in focus would require almost a complete revolution of the focus ring. Such a movement is very difficult indeed to carry out quickly and smoothly. A special optic known as the pack-shot lens is therefore made in which the focus ring movement is very much smaller for the same amount of focus shift as on an ordinary lens. It is also designed for extreme close range focus without supplementary attachments of any kind. Two typical pack-shot lenses are the Makro Kilar 40-mm $f2\cdot8$ with a focus range of 4 in. to infinity and the Makro Kilar 90-mm $f2\cdot8$ with a focus range of $5\frac{3}{8}$ in. to infinity.

While very satisfactory for their designed purpose these lenses would not be suitable for general photography because the focus is too highly geared for the precise and sometimes very slight adjustments needed during the course of an ordinary take. But they are certainly handy for extreme close shots where extension tubes might otherwise be necessary.

Wide-angle converter and tele-extender lenses

The wide-angle converter is a special lens made to fit over the front of a lens to reduce its magnification by shortening the focal length. It has normally been used with zoom lenses to provide a second range of focal lengths extending from a much wider angle initially. This dual range facility overcomes the problem with some zoom lenses—namely, that although they provide a true telephoto focal length the minimum setting may not be much wider than the "standard." Wide-angle converters have only the slightest effect on exposure, and the combination alters the depth of field at any setting to that for a conventional lens of the equivalent focal length. This type of lens, however, has tended to drop from general use in recent years, except the fisheye version which is normally fitted onto a 50-mm lens. But the fisheye effect is, of course, needed only very occasionally.

Certain forms of tele-extender lenses are manufactured for use with zoom lenses. They fit between the lens and the camera and in effect slightly open out the converging rays at the back of the lens so that they are made to focus at a point farther back than normal. The effect here is an increase in magnification throughout the zoom range, giving an extra long telephoto. Increase in focal length is in direct relation to the factor of the lens. A 2x extender doubles all focal lengths so that a 25–250-mm lens becomes 50–500 mm. This has a considerable effect on the exposure, requiring an increase of two stops or more according to the magnification factor of the tele-extender.

It is generally accepted, however, that any form of optical attachment is likely to have some effect on image quality, however slight.

Supplementary close-up lenses

A supplementary close-up or "diopter" lens is generally a meniscus lens that fits over the front of the camera lens. It allows close focusing at a range that varies according to its power, which is expressed in diopters, the reciprocal of the focal length in metres. The focal length of a lens in mm may be found by dividing 1000 by the quoted dioptric power of the lens. For example the focal length of a 2-diopter lens is:

$$\frac{1000}{2} \text{ or } 500 \text{ mm, i.e. } 50 \text{ cm}$$

When the camera lens is focused on infinity and the close-up lens is in position the lens will be focused on a point 50 cm from the lens. This is the maximum range because every camera lens can be focused nearer than infinity. For the closer focus ranges a correspondingly closer focus distance is possible with the close-up lens.

Generally, close-up lenses are not manufactured with very great magnifications because they would then cause a severe deterioration in film image quality. Lenses may be combined to give the equivalent of a stronger lens. In this case the dioptric powers are simply added together and the combined figure used as a basis for calculating their effect.

Split-field lenses

When a camera lens is focused on infinity or on objects at a considerable range, almost any subject in the immediate foreground will be so far out of focus at any normal working aperture that it may even be invisible. If a segment, or half of a close-up lens is placed in front of the camera lens it can bring nearby objects at one side of the picture into sharp focus yet retain focus on the distant subject filling the remainder. Thus the field is split into two "strips" of sharp focus while the intermediate range remains defocused.

A split-field lens is usually a half lens which can be positioned to cover half or less than half of the camera lens. A similar effect can, however, be obtained by shooting separate strips of film and having them combined in printing.

When small apertures are used on a wide-angle camera lens or zoom setting and a split field lens positioned correctly on a piece of close-up foreground, tremendous deep focus effects can be produced with every part of the picture rendered sharp.

The main problem with split-lens technique is to disguise the edge area joining the two fields. This may be done by lining it up on certain features in the scene. But the split-field lens can only be used where the particular circumstances allow adjustment or some scope for fitting the requirements of the lens to the scene.

Faceted lenses

A faceted lens produces a series of images of the subject in one frame by a system of internal prisms, which are normally arranged geometrically across the picture area. It is a very conscious "optical" effect and is normally reserved only for commercial or advertising film work.

Anamorphic lens

Anamorphosis is the application of horizontal compression to an image, used in a number of wide-screen systems. Anamorphic lenses

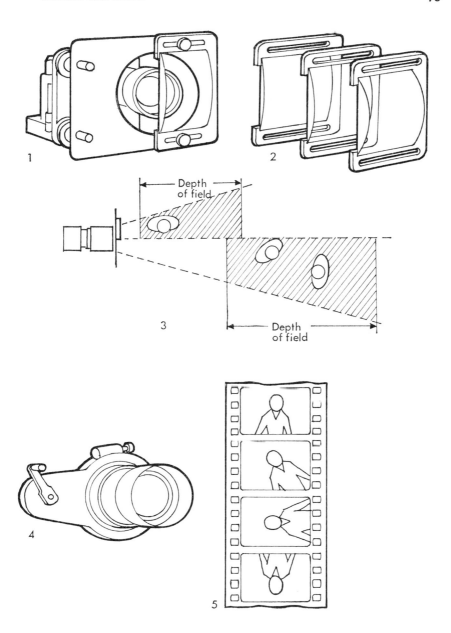

1, Split-field dioper lens is an arrangement which allows a supplementary close up lens, 2, to be positioned partly across the camera lens so that 3, parts of the scene at greatly varying ranges (beyond the normal available depth of field) may both be rendered sharp. The dividing line between the two areas may be disguised by lining it up with a straight feature in the scene or making it fall across a shadow area. 4, Rotator lens can reproduce static images upside down, sideways or at any angle 5, through 360°.

are usually supplied as part of a range produced for a certain system and the optical effect is in any event removed by the time the image appears on the screen. But anamorphotic effects have been used in screen images by deliberately missing out the decompression stage. Conventional uses of the anamorphic lens are discussed on page 41.

Rotating lens, or Dove prism

The whole film image may be turned on its side, upside down or at any angle in a full circle by a rotating lens which fits on to nearly any 35-mm camera. The lens rotates in either direction and is suitable for use with static scenes. It can be combined with a prismatic multi-image lens. It is, however, restrictive on the angle of lens that may be used while normally 50 mm is the longest acceptable focal length. It also results in a reversal of the picture left to right.

3

Lighting and Other Equipment

ARC LIGHTING, although involving heavy and cumbersome equipment which must be run from a DC supply provides such massive light output that despite those disadvantages it remains in wide use in larger film studios and on location where major productions are shot.

ARC LAMP PRINCIPLES

The principle of carbon arc illumination is very simple—a spark is maintained between positively and negatively charged points giving a brilliant white light. But the consistency of this illumination depends on the carbons having the correct polarity and separation. Without this the light tends to spit or flicker. As the arc burns, the carbon rods are gradually consumed and on average they last for an hour before they have to be replaced. The rods must be brought together as they shorten to maintain the constant gap, which on a 225-amp brute, is $\frac{3}{4}$ in. One carbon is moved toward the other electronically, although for extra adjustments it can be hand-operated. The two carbons are not placed end to end, but at an angle with the negative one beneath. To avoid uneven burning at the tip (crater) of the positive carbon (which is burned more quickly) as it moves forward it is also gradually rotated. The negative carbon does not need to be rotated.

The carbons can be seen through special heavily filtered viewing glasses at the sides and back of the lamp which reflect an image of the carbon tips through a mirror or prism system. There is a polarity light to show which way the current is flowing and the carbons are watched through the window to check that the right one burns first. If not, then polarity can be reversed.

Two kinds of positive carbon are used in these lamps. To vary the quality of illumination it is only necessary to modify the constituents of the carbon at the positive pole.

1. The low colour temperature (LCT) carbon gives light of a quality near to that of an incandescent lamp though, of course, of much higher intensity. The output is greater than that of a white flame carbon plus its filter. It burns at 3350 K. (These carbons are rarely used nowadays because they tend to flicker.)

2. The white flame carbon gives light of about 6000 K. To correct this for sunlight a gelatin filter (WF Green) white flame green is used over the lamp. To correct to incandescent light a colour temperature orange (CTO) filter is used. This corrects to approx. 3200 K.

The process of changing carbons in an arc lamp is known as "trimming" and takes no more than a minute to carry out. The inner section or mechanism of the lamp hinges back to provide access, and both carbon rods are replaced. There is a regulator at the back of this section to control the speed of rotation for the positive carbon.

Another control, the "spot and flood" selector, permits adjustments to the width of the light beam emitted from the lamp. This calibrates the spread of the beam on an index numbered 0–100, 100 being the full spot position and 0 being full flood. The cameraman calls out this setting to the chief electrician.

Arc Lamp Types

There are three main types of arc lamp: the brute, the 150-amp and the duarc.

The brute, a 225-amp focusing spot arc lamp, provides the basic illumination on all large-scale productions. A super brute (275 amp) has been used but has not been widely adopted. The heat output of the carbon arc is very considerable, so it is contained in a well-ventilated housing. The light is focused through a heat-resistant 25-in. diameter fresnel lens, and adjustment to the beam width is possible between 16° (spot) and 48° (flood) limits.

There is a difference in construction between brutes made in the US and those in the UK. American models are made in one piece, whereas British models have a removable centre section containing the carbons and their mountings. As a safety measure this section cannot be taken out unless the unit is switched off.

The 150-amp arc, though smaller and of lower output than a brute, is of the same basic design, with a 20-in. fresnel lens and a beam width adjustable between 3.5° (spot) and 10.5° (flood). The gap between the carbons is maintained at $\frac{1}{2}$ in. and, as with the brute there is power-operated carbon feed.

There is also a spot 150 arc producing a hard-outline focused spot effect sometimes used in filming theatre shows, but rarely applied to other film work.

The duarc or twin arc, a 40-amp soft field light, is an old type of lamp which is very seldom used nowadays. The unit was heavy and the illumination tended to flutter and spit and was generally rather difficult to keep burning properly.

300-AMP WATER-COOLED SPOT

An unusual unit is the 300-amp water-cooled spot lamp. This is a lensed light using a water supply of 15–20 lb pressure circulating through the jaws which hold the carbons. Such cooling is necessary because of the excessive heat emitted at this amperage. The lamp is used as a very high intensity follow-spot to dominate powerful lighting set-ups.

It takes two men to operate the lamp, one to follow the artist and the other to watch the volt and amp meters. The amperage is variable between 300 and 150 DC running off any 1000-amp generator.

For safety reasons, if the water supply is turned off the light automatically goes out. Additionally, a shutter is fitted between the carbon and the rear lens to prevent damage to the lens.

The size of the spot can be adjusted with a spread, or focus control, and also the intensity, by means of an iris on the front.

COLOUR CORRECTION FILTERS FOR ARC LAMPS

The white flame light can be adjusted spectrally to the equivalent of incandescent illumination by placing a gelatin colour temperature orange CTO filter over the front of the lamp. But with this there is a loss of light output in the order of 40 per cent.

The filters are available in various densities known as full, half or quarter grades.

Additionally, a Yl yellow or white flame green filter is used with white flame carbons to remove ultra-violet light content.

All colour correction filters used over powerful light sources tend to fade with time and should be checked and replaced when necessary.

DIFFUSING SCREENS

Diffusing screens are slotted into position immediately in front of the lamp, and are designed to withstand great heat. Two forms of diffuser are widely used—spun glass and Windolite. Spun glass is a translucent soft fibre-glass sheet material which can be put up like Windolite, which is sometimes called a "jelly" and is a gelatin screen with wire mesh in it. In the United States steel wire mesh diffusers are preferred. Spun glass reduces the light intensity to a much greater degree than Windolite and gives very soft diffusion. If more than one diffuser is needed it is better to use spun glass, as multiple layers of Windolite tend to give a yellow tinge to the light.

GENERATORS

As the carbon arc lamp is the main source of illumination for feature film work and requires a 115V DC supply, most studio and location power is at this pressure, though there has more recently been a move toward using AC for work in interiors where small AC-working iodine-quartz lights are more convenient than the bulky alternatives.

Low voltage equipment is safer for complex lighting rigs and the shorter lamp filaments are more able to withstand vibration and shock from handling. Against this, the power cables and ancillary equipment are quite heavy.

Studios use power from the national or commercial grid supply, converting for the equipment in the studio, but they generally also have a standby generating plant for extra demand, or where peak period consumption affects the outside supply.

Much of the power in the small studio comes from overhead grids, confining the number of cables crossing the floor to equipment actually used on the floor. Generators in the studio power house and those used on location are generally diesel, developing DC. Some AC generators are manufactured for lightweight work and these are usually petrol-driven 130-amp 240-V (mobile), or 45-amp (portable) generators weighing only 17 cwt. There are also 150- and 200-amp DC lightweight generators.

Nowadays, there is much effort to make mobile generators silent running if possible. This is important for two reasons. First, the unit is often working in residential areas at night and, secondly, reduced noise makes it possible to place the generator nearer the shooting area. Soundproofing in a generator normally consists of two layers of mineral wall. Small generators tend to be more noisy than the larger ones and insulation for them is much heavier. But nowadays for heavy duty work 1000-amp generators are used in preference to 2000-amp which for practical purposes have not proved so successful. Two 1000-amp machines can be used with the load divided between them and placed one on either side of the set so that the cables can be kept clear. As each brute draws 225 amp, four can be run off each generator.

One of the problems with running the older type of generator was that the voltage had to be constantly watched, and it was a full-time job for someone to sit and check the output from dials on the unit. Occasionally, if the arc lights were killed first, incandescent lamps sharing the same power supply blew with the sudden rise in voltage. Nowadays generators have automatically controlled voltage and speed so the lamps can be killed in any order. Although automatic control is a great advantage for efficient operation, failure is not entirely eliminated because the unforeseeable snag such as a fuel blockage might still occur. In this case nowadays, the first indication that something is wrong is that the lights fail.

There is no hard-and-fast figure for a suitable distance from the working area at which to place a modern generator. About 200 or 300 ft is an average minimum but this depends on the peculiarities of the site chosen. For example, in traffic scenes where the general noise level drowns the generator it could be as close as 50 ft to the site.

A special mobile lighting unit for location work is the self-mobilized brute. This consists of a Land-Rover fitted with a generator and a brute positioned on a platform above the cab. The platform can be raised and lowered. The generator develops 250 amp.

TYPES OF INCANDESCENT LIGHTING

The incandescent lights used in film work are of two main types, focusing (lensed) lights and open (flood) units.

The main focusing lamps are the Tenner (10 kW) the largest incandescent lamp in general use, the Senior (5 kW), the Junior (2 kW), the Pup (750 W) and the Inkie Dinkie (100–200 W).

The Tenner has a 20-in-diameter fresnel lens and allows beam adjustment from 16° to 46°. It is usually mounted on a braced tripod with castors and an adjustable centre column.

The Senior with a 14-in. fresnel lens has a beam variable between 13° and 60° and is similarly mounted to the Tenner.

The Junior, with a 10-in. lens and 12–44° beam width, is mounted on an adjustable column with leg members and castors.

The Pup and Inkie Dinkie are versions of the same lamp on a very much reduced scale.

Various types of open light are manufactured, all basically with a bowl-type reflector, some deep shaped and others shallow.

A basher, used mainly for low key work, is supplied in various sizes from 200 to 500 W.

The Skypan is a very widely used type of unit. It has a wide shallow circular reflector, and gives a soft spread of light over a very wide area. It is fitted with a 5- or 10-kW bubble (bulb) and is often used to light backings in the studio. It is normally supported on a tubular leg stand on castors.

The cone light is a lamp of fairly light construction giving soft

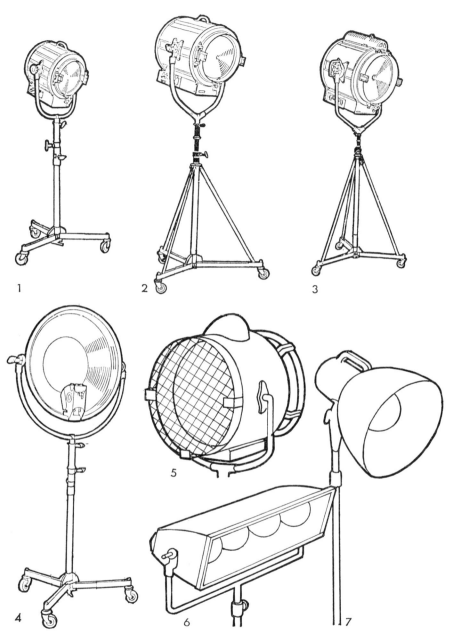

Typical incandescent and a carbon arc lighting. 1, Junior, a 2K incandescent lamp with a fresnel lens giving adjustable beam angle (12-44°); 2, Senior 5K incandescent lamp with fresnel lens and beam adjustment (13–60°); 3, Tenner 10K high-power incandescent lamp with fresnel lens and adjustable beam angle (16–46°); 4, Skypan, a 5K incandescent wide angle flood lamp in an aluminium reflector (170°) often used for lighting backdrops; 5 Brute, standard 225 amp arc lamp for motion picture work with fresnel lens and beam adjustment (16–48°) also in a 150-amp version; 6, Quad, floodlight with four 250- or 500-W incandescent bulbs for general purpose or frontal lighting; 7, Scoop 500- or 1000-W incandescent flood light.

field illumination and is used in the studio on a stand, or hung on a spigot. It is made in 2- and 5-kW versions.

A can light is an open can reflector containing two 1000-W bulbs and fitted with a frosted glass diffuser which softens the light.

Any of these lamps may be removed from its stand and mounted on overhead supports, special rigging, etc.

Tungsten Halogen Illumination

For many years it has been the wish of both the manufacturers and users of motion picture lighting equipment to attain lighter and more compact construction without losing the high light output necessary for today's working conditions and materials.

A light source relatively new to the industry, which has a high output for its size and weight is the tungsten halogen lamp (also known as quartz iodine, or tungsten iodine). The lamp has a normal tungsten filament but is filled with a halogen gas (usually, but not essentially iodine). This type of lamp will burn for a long time without discolouring because particles from the burning filament, instead of being distributed on the inside of the envelope in the normal way are redeposited on the filament itself. This process also lengthens the life of the filament, though, admittedly, the deposit is not distributed evenly over it. The immense heat from these bulbs requires that the envelope be made from heat-resistant material. Originally quartz was used, but this has generally now been superseded by a special toughened glass.

Mini brute

This is a square frame containing nine tungsten halogen dichroic bulbs of 100 W each, and is used as a fill light, offering the usual control of barn doors and slot for inserting spun-glass diffusers. Each lamp on the unit may be switched on independently. It is rated at approximately 600 ft candles at 12 ft (i.e. about twice the output of a skypan). It burns for 16 hours but is more expensive to run than a brute because of the replacement cost of the lamps.

North Light

Another tungsten iodine unit using four 1000-W lamps, it gives a light output somewhat similar to a 5-kW cone light, i.e. a soft field.

Fresnel Lenses

Lamps having fresnel lenses at the front are subject to damage in wet working conditions as water falling on a hot fresnel lens can crack it. The lens should always be shielded as much as possible from the rain or spray when working near water.

LIGHTING ACCESSORIES

Gobo is the term for a black piece of wood or similar material mounted on a frame that can be positioned in front of a lamp to shade off a part of the set from the light. It can be totally opaque or rather less so, either to shade off or just cut the illumination down to a definite shape in a particular area of the set. It might be a straight-shaped device which is pushed in front of a lamp so that the light is cut off in a straight line down the edge of a wall for example. Or it can have a curved shape which casts a soft shadow over a section of the room. Gobos and flags are indispensable and there should be a good supply of them in the studio.

A *flag* is a square or rectangular piece of board on a stand which can be moved about to shade a lamp off a part of the set that it should not strike. They are made in several different sizes affixed to rods with swivel joints that fit into "sentry" stands which have a fairly heavy base. They can be adjusted to various angles and directions and then locked. A "French flag" is a small one that can be screwed onto the side of a lamp and bent round. Enormous flags, say 15 ft wide, can be suspended by adjustable ropes from the roof of the studio to cut off completely a whole string of lights. Girders run the whole length of the studio and from these, lighting rails or even sets can be hung. A light such as a brute is so heavy that pantograph supports could not be used. With a studio measuring 200 ft by 100 ft and 40–50 ft high sometimes entirely filled by the set, lamps used to light such an area must be larger than those in a television studio. The heavy duty lighting rails can take brutes and 10-kW lamps. A film studio is in some ways more old-fashioned than a TV studio but it deals with much greater weights. A brute weighs 2–3 cwt complete. The lamps are hauled up on pulleys and put onto the rail.

Brute shutters are available for 150-amp lamps. They are like a Venetian blind fitted over the front of the lamp and can be quickly opened or closed for a flashing light effects.

An ulcer is a board with patterned shapes cut into it placed in the light beam to break up the light. This gives patterned effects which on some models can be revolved.

Yashmac is Windolite in an L-shaped frame clamped on to a stand and used for softening light on a part of the subject.

A *Molevator* is an electrically (115V AC/DC) geared lamp stand suitable for a brute or smaller lamp, which extends to 14 or 15 ft and saves time in handling. They run on three wheels (though there are some four-wheel versions) which can be locked off. The stand can also be folded.

A *Desert dolly* accepts a brute mounted on a Molevator or similar stand and is used for tracking the lamp during shooting or transporting it to a predetermined position over rough terrain. It has balloon tyred wheels on a lightweight tubular frame and is steered by a towing bar.

FILTERS AND SCREENS

The camera mattebox is normally provided with a rigid filter holder of some description. The filters are 6·6 in. square. Pola screens, however, fit into a rotating holder so that they may be positioned most favourably to cut out polarized light reflected from the subject, or to modify the sky rendering where polarized light in the sky allows this corrective treatment.

Basic kinds of filter are:

1 Those used in black and white photography to modify tone tendering by adjustment of the tone values of certain colours in the scene
2 Filters which reduce polarized light (pola filters or screens) and also control sky rendering with colour film where of course coloured filters could not be employed
3 Neutral density (ND) filters having a certain density of grey in the glass which reduces exposure without disturbing colour balance
4 *Graduated* neutral density filters which shade gradually top to bottom, beginning with the full density rating and diminishing to clear glass at the bottom
5 Colour correction filters designed to adjust the colour rendition of film to the nature of light by which it is exposed
6 Diffusion screens which provide various degrees of diffusion or halo effects in the image so that the highlight areas tend to spill over into the darker or shadow portions of the image, and detail (in the face, for instance) is softened and suppressed
7 Fog filters which give the impression of the natural atmospheric effect either by totally artificial means or by augmenting the natural effect.

PRACTICAL APPLICATIONS OF FILTERS

Filters for black and white

These are far less often necessary nowadays in full-scale productions. Some major production companies now think in terms of colour only. With the spread in colour television broadcasting in recent years, audiences have grown to expect colour, and if in any country television represents a significant secondary market for film, then that demand will be for colour productions also.

Filters for black and white photography are made from dyed glass or from gelatin sheets sandwiched between two optical flats. They are made in a wide range of colours both for effects and corrective purposes.

Corrective treatment serves to improve the tone gradation in the film image when the colours of the subject are of similar brightness. The aim is to achieve a good-quality image with a wide range of well-differentiated greys in the mid-tone for scenes where this quality is important.

It is not always an advantage to improve the image quality in this way; it very much depends upon the story. If the script seems to indicate that a lack of sky tone, for example, would suit the scene, then not only is corrective treatment not carried out but the opposite, a deliberate devaluing of tone may be what the director is looking for. On the other hand, a pale blue sky over a foliated scene can often have too much overall contrast. A light yellow filter would darken the sky a little and lighten the foliage, so tying them together more closely, tonally speaking. This is corrective treatment.

A deep orange or red filter darkens the blue in the sky to near black, the clouds remain white and the total effect is dramatic and unreal—effective treatment.

Polarizing screens

Used largely with colour film, the polarizing screen can influence the tonal rendering of parts of a scene lit by polarized light. Polarized light vibrates in one plane only relative to the axis of a light beam, as opposed to normal light vibrations which radiate in all directions at right angles to this axis.

A pola screen has a crystalline structure that transmits light vibrating in one plane only. Many light-reflecting surfaces polarize light striking them at certain angles also, and in nature parts of the sky are polarized relative to the position of the sun.

If a polarizing screen is positioned with its polarity at right angles to that of the polarized reflections from the subject, the reflections can be reduced to an extent depending on the shooting angle. Only light reflected at an angle of about 55° to the norm is totally polarized, so the maximum reduction of reflection is obtained when the camera is at about 35° to the reflecting surface. By rotating the screen, tone in certain areas of the sky can be modified, while subject colours remain unaffected. Reflections from certain objects in the scene, cars, shop windows, water, can be reduced by adjusting a pola screen to the opposite polarity. Polarizers placed in front of one another and rotated until one is at right angles to the other can fade the scene and finally cut the light altogether.

NEUTRAL DENSITY FILTERS

The ND filter reduces the overall brightness of the scene, and being grey, does not disturb the colour balance. A primary use for this type of filter is where the camera team is working under exceptionally bright conditions and the film would be unavoidably overexposed. Often it is used to give more control in a given situation by increasing the exposure necessary although cameras with adjustable shutters do much the same thing. If selective focus is required in a well-lit scene, the correct aperture setting may indicate a greater depth of field than required. With an ND filter the lens aperture must be opened. This gives the selective control necessary.

Graduated filters

These are designed for outdoor use to adjust the relative brightnesses of sky and scene to one another and so lower the contrast range of the scene as a whole. Greatest filter density corresponds to the sky area and in some situations where a bright sky is combined with a dark landscape it is possible to gain more detail in the landscape without overexposing the sky. Where the scene does not have such extreme contrast the filter can darken the sky without unduly influencing objects or scenery in the bottom of the frame.

In colour, where an overexposed sky might otherwise become quite colourless it can be separately controlled with the graduated filter. The upper part of the sky would appear darker blue, becoming lighter toward the horizon as it does in nature. The middle distance might be slightly darker and the foreground virtually unaffected. One disadvantage is that the filter is usually suitable only for shots not involving camera movement. If the camera were moved the gradation of density would become distinctly visible, moving across the scene like a cloud and cause a great imbalance in exposure. Graduated filters are available in various density ranges, and a set of three such filters is standard. They may be graded ND3 to clear, ND6 to clear, ND9 to clear, etc. This figure indicates the maximum factor of neutral density graduating to clear glass.

Colour correction filters

When a film is exposed under lighting conditions not designed for it, the bias in resultant colour rendering can be controlled by the use of a correction filter. A film designed for photography in tungsten lighting shows a blue bias when used outdoors and therefore requires a relatively strong amber filter to be placed over the camera lens. In the case of Eastmancolor negative material this filter would be the Wratten No. 85. Where mixed light sources of different colour values are used, say tungsten studio lamps and arc lights or daylight and the film is designed for tungsten, the light provided by the arc lights would prove unnaturally blue. The treatment here must be selective. Amber (No. 85) filters could be placed over the arcs to correct the imbalance, or special amber sheeting over the windows in the case of daylight.

Any filtering results in some light loss but this can be compensated by adequate studio lighting.

More subtle use of colour correction is made with photography outdoors at different times of the day when the value of daylight changes. Corrections are made toward or away from morning or evening effect with the slightly pinkish light (see page 200).

Diffusion screens

Although the effect of diffusion like so many effects can nowadays be introduced in printing on many occasions where on-the-spot diffusion effects are required a screen is used in front of the lens. This may be a fine gauze screen or a glass screen with some form of light-dispersing surface. Some such screens, having a clear centre will take effect only when used with the camera lens near maximum aperture. Broad diffusion effects can be obtained with other devices but very frequently a cameraman has his own ideas on obtaining diffused effects.

Fog filters

Fog filters or screens, placed over the lens, may be combined with fog produced by special effects and with appropriate lighting. They are an additive to the effect and as with other kinds of filter can be added by degrees. A set of three or four such fog filters of various densities could provide an exact match for the circumstances. Certainly on many occasions the natural effect of fog is improved for photography by placing a fog screen over the lens. In other cases a heavy fog screen over the lens could look very artificial with the wrong scene.

A fog filter is a glass disc ground on one face and treated with a laminate. The diffusion is characterized by a spread of diffused highlights over the darker areas. There is also some loss in definition. "Double fog" filters are specially designed to give the required veiling over the scene without loss of definition.

4

The Film—Preliminaries

AT THE BEGINNING of a film, the producer, who has already chosen his director, may ask him who he would like as cameraman on the film. The director has a choice and perhaps has somebody already in mind. He tells the producer who contacts the cameraman's agent. The agent gets in touch with the cameraman and arranges an interview. The cameraman goes up to see the director and/or the producer in an office or hotel room in London, or wherever they operate from, and eventually they give him a script to read to see if he would like to do it. Terms are discussed with the agent and a contract drawn up.

There are usually several discussions before the film starts and perhaps a few tests are made of some of the chosen actors and tests of make-up and costumes. For salary reasons, the cameraman is not usually taken on until just before the picture goes onto the floor. During preliminary discussions he is told the scheduled time of the picture, say ten or twelve weeks or six months, and also if it involves going abroad. Salary is based on the budget of the film. He might choose a film which pays less if he likes the director and feels the film will make an interesting job, and is attracted by the subject and location. A cameraman should be interested in the subject matter of a film he is going to work on. If he has various offers to choose from, it is quite natural that he should choose the subject he prefers.

PRELIMINARY TESTS

A week before production the cameraman may be called upon to make some preliminary tests—perhaps on a daily basis. It will be mostly testing make-up and costumes. There may be several different materials to choose between for various costumes and he might take shots of selected pieces of material hanging together so that the costume designer knows how they are going to photograph. This applies particularly if the film is going to be in colour. Some colours do not photograph the way they look; they may come out a little more brilliant than expected, or a yellow might become more of an orangey-yellow rather than a lemon-yellow. It is worth doing these tests beforehand, so that expensive costumes are not made up in the wrong colours. The colour of the costumes must be related in some way to the colours of the set, so the art director is vitally interested in the colours of costumes. He carries out similar colour tests on the set by painting only a small section of the set first, and having it photographed before painting the rest. The director may dislike a colour. These tests are to help the whole team who are making a picture—the cameraman, the costume designer, the set designer, the director and make-up people. The colours must blend harmoniously.

Pre-Production Conference

Some groups of film makers like to have a production conference before the film starts. A typical procedure with major American companies is to call a pre-production conference where everybody meets to discuss the film and all the problems involved. There would probably be as many as fifteen people round the table, including the director, the production manager, the art director, the cameraman, the costume designer, the set dresser, the property man, etc. The art director might be asked for an estimate of what the sets will cost for the whole picture. They all have a chance to air their views and bring up any points that might be of interest before everybody becomes involved in making the picture. Notes are taken of these to avoid the risk of any small or large calamity taking place after the picture has been started. Calling such a general conference is not common practice now but it still happens with some groups of film makers.

The Script

The script that is given to the cameraman is usually rough and still being improved upon. The final version does not generally emerge until the very last moment. This revision often goes on all through the picture. At times the director may call in the scriptwriter to rewrite a certain scene.

Some years ago people working for major American companies would be told, when handed the script, that it was the final version and must not be altered, even by a word in the dialogue, for instance. If, at any time, during the film, the director or leading actor wanted to change a word they had to contact the producer or phone his office and ask permission, explaining why they wanted to change it. This was not considered restrictive because the film company was determined to save money and time. Today, the director is more important than in the days when he was the employee of a major company and could be simply given his marching orders. Nowadays he has a much freer hand.

The script very seldom contains instructions for lighting or camera work although the scriptwriter sometimes gives a sketchy indication of his own ideas, i.e. night, day, dawn, evening or nightclub with smoke-laden atmosphere, but no actual lighting directions. Most such decisions usually come from the director or the cameraman.

If, however, the film is taken from a novel, a dramatic lighting effect suggested by the original story might be retained in the script and subsequently used in the scene as it is shot.

Suitable lighting for the scene is always decided upon before the shooting starts. When the cameraman looks at the script he thinks in terms of mental pictures—how he is going to light it. He sees opportunities which he discusses with the director, bearing in mind the effect that the director is trying to convey.

LOOKING FOR LOCATIONS

In reconnoitring for a suitable location the director is accompanied by an art director, cameraman and perhaps the production manager. The director has the final say and, although the choice is really his, the site must be a practical one usable by the art director and camera-man. Before looking at a location himself a director may send a stills photographer from the studio to shoot material that he can analyse. Stills can serve only as a rough idea for the team, to indicate where further investigation might be made. Yard rules and/or the human figure seen in the stills give a reasonable idea of scale, and further photographs may be taken from which the art director might work to reproduce a feature such as a doorway. These would indicate exact measurements and close-ups would be used to record the texture of the subject, which will be copied exactly. Both the cameraman and art director will naturally be concerned about the space available at the location and whether it is sufficient for the action and camera position, especially if additional parts are to be constructed. The still camera is not used for any indication of the eventual camera positions; they will be decided by the director later on.

Before moving in on an area, and in fact, before much planning has been done, the production manager needs permission from the owner of the property and must consult the police or any other people directly or indirectly concerned. Fees usually have to be paid and arrangements made for making good any damage such as the relaying of lawns. During a second reconnoitre with the cameraman, notes are made of the facilities for erecting platforms for lighting and shooting.

But the whole question of camera position must remain fluid so that the director can make up his mind as he is shooting which angle he will use. The team may at this time be visiting other locations that will be used in the film including streets and alleys, a spot on the Thames Embankment or the inside of a theatre. Applications for the use of all these places and other arrangements may keep the production manager busy for weeks. The second reconnoitre involves the chief electrician and construction manager. Shots are definitely pinpointed and positions finalized for lighting rostrums by the cameraman. He draws up a plan that may require say a 64-ft tower in one place and a tubular rostrum on the far side of a canal or over the roof of a garage. The lighting plan may indicate a brute at 18 ft in one place and one at 14 ft in another. The cameraman makes a list of all equipment he will need on this job. The construction manager makes a plan of the various parts to be erected and the electrician does likewise, at the same time finding a place to put his generators, if possible, out of earshot. The construction manager is also in charge of building parts of the set, working directly from the art director's plans. The art director has noted the cameraman's requirements as well as the director's. The cameraman may want a lamp-post or a lantern hanging from the wall for a certain lighting effect.

The constructors have to start work well in advance of the first shooting day. When seeking locations in a foreign country one may often work from scratch with no previous groundwork except information about the kind of terrain to be found in certain areas. It may be necessary for the cameraman and director to travel a thousand miles or so back and forth through a country to find suitable locations, some of which might be in towns or villages and others in remote areas.

Historical backgrounds may be constructed or searched for. There are certain streets in London, for example, which have changed little over the last couple of hundred years. Perhaps part of the street only can be used and the camera viewpoint is arranged to include only that part. Some modern street furniture may be disguised by the art director using old signs, street features, traffic, people, etc. If the street has changed too much, old prints may help the art director in constructing a mock street in the studio or on the outdoor lot. The mock street would be full size but there may be a slight perspective effect at the far end giving a greater feeling of distance. The first 100 ft or so would be full size. The street would begin to rise in the latter part and so people could not appear in it. Although it may go on for another 50–100 ft it might give the effect of 300 yds; the houses at the far end may be only one-third natural size. If people had to appear, children dressed as adults could stand in this part of the street.

ORDERING EQUIPMENT

Immediately the planning of a picture is under way the production manager asks the director of photography what lighting is required. Having read the script and made notes he decides on all the lighting equipment needed for the picture.

The cameraman also states which equipment he will need for given periods of the production, i.e. on location or in the studio where the requirements are quite different. The studio has its own permanent lighting source, the power house. Studio light comes partially from the grid system via a conversion to DC. AC is rarely used in a studio for film lighting because of the safety factor—open plug boxes and connectors are lethal with AC. DC is required for carbon arc lamps in any case and is more convenient for heavy loads as a single stage may have outlets for 5000 amp at 115V DC. The cameraman states the required lighting in units. When on location he will need mobile generators. A 1000-amp generator will just run four brutes as each one takes 225 amp. (The power of arc lamps is referred to by the amperage consumed, not by their kilowatt value.) He might need twelve or twenty brutes. For other equipment the cameraman employs whatever is available at the studio unless the film calls for some very unusual piece of equipment that the studio does not hold in stock. Cameras, however, are frequently hired from another source, especially cameras for particular processes such as Panavision, where some equipment is never sold but hired out by the manufacturer.

A special crane or other equipment might be required for a certain sequence. Following discussions between the director and the cameraman the production department would hire the item from a concern specializing in such equipment. Equipment can be hired for, say, a day or a week or for longer periods, depending on the requirements of the production. For productions which are being shot abroad he might hire a number of freelance men. He might have a freelance cameraman and sound man who bring in freelance crews and equipment which does not belong to any studio. Sound equipment might be owned by the sound man himself and in this case in addition to salary he would require a hire fee for the equipment which is used in making the film. He might hire a very expensive crane which he must carry for the duration of the picture or the larger part of the picture. In London this equipment would be too expensive to hire for longer than the exact time it was needed. The cost of carrying every foreseeable item of equipment necessary on a remote location tends to restrict this type of operation to productions in which such costs can be off-set against the absence of studio rental. In the case of remote locations, such as in a desert, expensive equipment may be on loan for many months.

ORDERING FILM STOCK

All film stock is ordered in one batch for a colour production. The amount that will be needed is decided by the director, cameraman and production manager. If the picture is going to take three months to shoot, the production manager will know from experience that for three months' work on a certain type of film 200,000 ft of film would be needed. The manufacturer is then asked to reserve a batch of, say, 300,000 ft of one emulsion. This is to ensure that there is no variation in colour quality through the film, because all the stock will have been made at one period and consequently shares the same characteristics whatever they may be. Slight variations from one batch to another do occur, and for a major colour production all possibility of uneven quality must be eliminated.

The manufacturer supplies a sample of a given batch to test and the stock is then reserved. It very seldom happens that the film is not suitable at all, but it could have some fault such as a stress mark or spottiness. Where additional material is required the manufacturer will test a further batch for similar characteristics.

The choice of camera stock is not a very wide one. In England and the USA, Eastman film is very widely used for colour work. Eastman Kodak and Ilford offer a range of slow, medium and fast monochrome materials, and additionally Agfa Gevaert films are used in Belgium, France and Germany. Monochrome materials are now no longer in wide use.

Major productions are most often shot on Eastmancolor. The names of special colour processes, such as Metrocolor, De Luxe Color, etc., that often appear on credit titles are the studio or laboratory printing processes, all of course based on the standard Eastmancolor negative stock manufactured by Kodak. The present emulsion in use is 5254, the manufacturer's reference number.

PLANNING SHOOTING SEQUENCE

Shooting is planned on the most convenient and economically sensible basis. Shots using one location are naturally all grouped together in that part of the filming schedule. If the unit is not in some remote place far from home, any special equipment which is very expensive to hire is used within the shortest period possible so that it is not idle while building up hire charges.

These considerations are planned as far as possible by the production manager. But, of course, overruling all such considerations is the availability of main stars. Shots involving them on location are grouped together, and they may have to fit in with other commitments at the end of their contract period when they might have been engaged to begin another picture. Crowd scenes which can be highly expensive, arrangements with non-film organizations, church authorities or the armed forces for example, may also have to fit into certain dates, or because of prior arrangement be unalterable to suit a film company that happens to be behind on its shooting schedule. These factors making up a jig-saw puzzle of possible arrangements must be weighed up economically and from a practical standpoint so that an overall plan is produced. This is all the responsibility of the production manager. A cameraman can offer advice as to how he can manage with given resources at a given time and his requirements are obviously very prominent here.

Location and studio work are two separate parts of the working programme. Customarily, the location work is done first if there is a substantial amount, but in unfavourable weather conditions or less favourable times of the year for particular locations the studio sequences might be embarked on beforehand. Studio shots being more controllable in so many respects offer scope for "tailoring" supporting shots to fit with existing location material. Working the reverse procedure tends to remove this franchise.

The shots are grouped for various parts of the schedule and, working with a handful at a time, the various departments bring in their own contributions for the scene. The production manager checks that all equipment and facilities the cameraman has asked for are there at the time they are needed. It is for the cameraman to check that they function, do the job properly and are ready when the shot is tried. The cameraman checks that he has the necessary lights but it is the chief electrician who must see that they are in proper working order and provide substitutes if they are not. He must also ensure that they are brought into the right place at the right time by his crew of electricians and grips.

Various departments make their own production notes about the equipment, scenery, costumes, props, etc., needed for each shot, using the shooting script and schedule as a basis. In this way everything should come together smoothly, with each person carrying out his jobs immediately each shot is completed, in preparation for the next. When a team is working smoothly it is noticeable that the next set-up takes shape with comparatively few words being spoken. Briefed beforehand, everyone just moves swiftly into place. The basics of the shot are thus prepared and leave time for adjustments by the director or his cameraman.

5

Lighting Objectives and Procedure

SOMETIMES, when a scene is held together by dialogue between two persons, the pictorial side of the film becomes, for that moment at least, temporarily subordinated. Directors are often content to rely on the interest of what is said or the conflicting personalities of the individuals portrayed. Nevertheless, such scenes, although mostly dialogue, can often be improved considerably by the atmosphere imparted to the scene in the photography. Much excitement can be added to a scene by the lighting treatment, which can help convince the audience of the truth of what they are witnessing. To gain authenticity it is almost a duty of the cameraman to imply in his work much more than is just in the script. Of course, it is essential that the atmosphere the cameraman tries to create is the correct one. When working in conjunction with the art director some most striking effects can be obtained which are not suggested by a rather ordinary script. A director is often happy to have suggestions from a cameraman as to how a scene of this nature could be improved. Even a small action, such as switching on a light might serve to sustain the interest by giving an actor a natural bit of business to do in an otherwise static scene.

PRIOR ARRANGEMENTS AND INSPECTION

Large indoor sets are usually planned well in advance and possibly without reference to the cameraman's requirements. His first glimpse of a large and complete set may be during an odd half-hour's break from work on another scene.

With some forethought, the art director can design a set to suit possible lighting requirements. For any detailed work he would naturally benefit from consultation with the cameraman. A small section of the set may be made removable so that a hidden lamp may be used

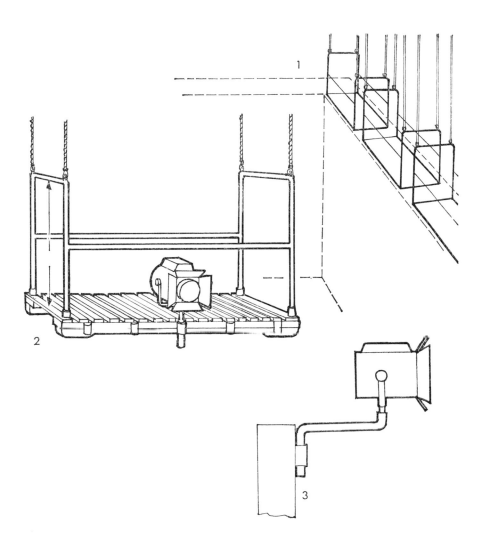

Lamps may be mounted on "chairs" above the set. 1, They are of tubular steel construction with boards across the base and lamp spigots on the side. 2, When rigged side by side they provide a continuous catwalk round the top of the set allowing free access to the lamps mounted on them. 3, Chairs are usually suspended from the ceiling by ropes and bolted to the top of the set for rigidity.

to simulate light from a visible light source. A removable panel may allow another lamp to be lowered into the best position for a certain shot. Various shots on this same set may require changes in lighting and ideally allowances for all these should be made in its design.

Modifications when the shooting takes place in a real house are necessarily limited. The ceiling cannot be removed, but you are still required to light the set in the appropriate mood. Lighting from outside can be done in a similar way to that in a studio set. A tower might be built outside the house with a powerful light directed through the window to simulate sunlight.

Looking over the set, preferably with the director, art director and chief electrician, the cameraman tries to find out from the director where he wants to start and any particular ideas he may have about the scenes to be shot.

While consulting his script beforehand, the cameraman should have formed mental pictures of how he intends to light the scene and, in fact, the film in general. The lighting must, of course, suit the scene and correspond with the effect that the director is trying to convey.

Bearing all this in mind, he may check with the art director that adequate provision has been made for lighting and suggest any improvements that seem necessary. Then he can issue precise instructions to the chief electrician for the position of lighting rails and types of lamp that will be valuable or necessary for the lighting ideas which have by now formed in his mind. Extra rails and equipment are placed in positions prior to the shooting day to cover all possible aspects arising from this preliminary survey.

An art director may discuss any light fittings or "practicals" (to appear in an indoor scene) with the cameraman beforehand and agree on two or three shades from a larger selection taking into consideration the power of actual lamps to be used in them. If an oil lamp were to be used, the cameraman may ask for one with a double wick to give a stronger flame or possibly have it wired up for an electric bulb, which, however, must be disguised by the shade. The script may require that the lamp be carried about the room. A trailing flex would not do if it were supposed to be an oil lamp, and a battery may not produce sufficient illumination for the extra light needed for colour photography. A property man could find some lamps and one of these would be adapted to take a double wick. Sometimes a double wick is put into a candle too, to give a brighter effect.

First Lighting at Rehearsals

On the first day of shooting the actors may be called on for rehearsal before work begins, allowing them time for dressing and

Premiere of *Lawrence of Arabia*, Odeon Leicester Square, 1962, Freddie Young being presented to H.M. The Queen.

Page 98 (Top) *Sixty Glorious Years* (1938—Herbert Wilcox) with Anna Neagle and Anton Walbrook. Freddie taking light reading. (Bottom) *The Conspirator* (1949—MGM, Victor Saville) Robert Taylor in tube train at Aldwych, London.

Page 99 (Top) *Edward, My Son* (1948—MGM) Director George Cukor, Spencer Tracy, and Freddie Young on Thames Embankment. (Bottom) *Bhowani Junction* (1956—MGM, George Cukor) smelly location in Lahore, Pakistan.

Page 100 (Top) *Lawrence of Arabia* (1961—Horizon/Columbia) Taking reading, with inquisitive camel, and (Bottom) crawling up sand dune to spot a camera angle.

Page 101 (Top) *Seventh Dawn* (1963—Columbia) Location, Malaya. Director Lewis Gilbert, with William Holden and Freddie Young reading cable from Hollywood after Oscar Award for *Lawrence of Arabia*. (Bottom) *Lord Jim* (1964—Columbia, Richard Brooks) Camera on raft: with operator Ernie Day, focus Ken Withers and clapper loader Bobbie Stillwell. How to get a sun tan and be paid for it.

Page 102 (Top) *Lord Jim* Aberdeen, Hong Kong; sampans and floating Community Town. (Bottom) *Nicholas and Alexandra* (1971—Horizon/Columbia). Freddie Young with director Franklin Schaffner, on steps in Madrid Station, arrival of train for troops waiting to go to the Front.

Page 103 (Top) *Ryan's Daughter* (1969–70—MGM) Freddie Young with director David Lean on crane in tree tops for wood scene. (Bottom) Lining up through clear screen for the storm sequence.

Page 104 *Ryan's Daughter*, watching a rehearsal in the pub.

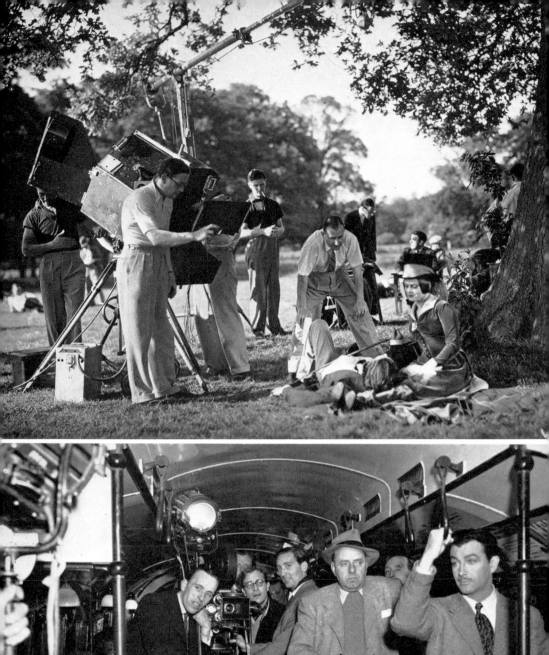

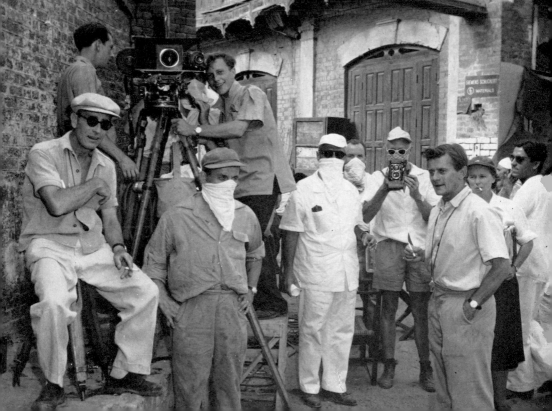

make-up later. This period is useful for making arrangements and perhaps putting on a few lamps for a little rudimentary lighting around the set. This "roughing in" of lighting does not confine a cameraman to the various positions chosen.

Normally when the actors arrive on the set, the first thing necessary for everyone is a rehearsal. This may last an hour or two, until the director is satisfied. The actors then move off and the cameraman completes the lighting with stand-ins who take up the various positions and movements that the actors have rehearsed. This is a rehearsal for lighting and camera movement, microphone movement and for any ancilliary persons who are also involved with the scene. In this way everyone can be quite certain of what is going to happen when the scene is shot. The actors then come on again and the first take is tried.

There are no hard-and-fast rules about lighting a set. The cameraman tries to make some preparations beforehand but quite often he goes onto the set without any pre-lighting. He may have rails with lights all the way round the set and in every conceivable position. At this stage, of course, the lights have not been switched on.

It may take several rehearsals for a scene before the director hits upon the right idea for playing it, and the cameraman can then start lighting in earnest. So a scene cannot be preplanned in detail. It may all have to be changed because the director's final idea does not correspond exactly with the script, and the cameraman's original conception of the lighting.

INDOOR LIGHTING—GENERAL PROCEDURE

As a rule, the cameraman does a fairly general lighting of the set, covering the wall area, and then lights it for the positions of the actors. As they may subsequently move in nearly every possible direction about the set he always plans a general lighting scheme which avoids as far as possible lights not well placed for these movements. He can light the walls satisfactorily without laying himself open to difficulties when the actor comes on. The rehearsal tells him roughly what is going to happen, certainly far more exactly than any script is able to.

He normally starts with his main or key light and works down to the shadows. These he can play around with by eye, as they are usually well outside the scope of a meter reading.

In a certain set up the key light might come from high up where the actual light or lighting in the room would normally be. This lights the wall but actors' shadows fall down behind them, clearing them for movement. Fill in can come from diffused open lights and effects lights can enliven particular areas of the background where a table lamp or wall light or domestic spotlight were supposed to be positioned. An

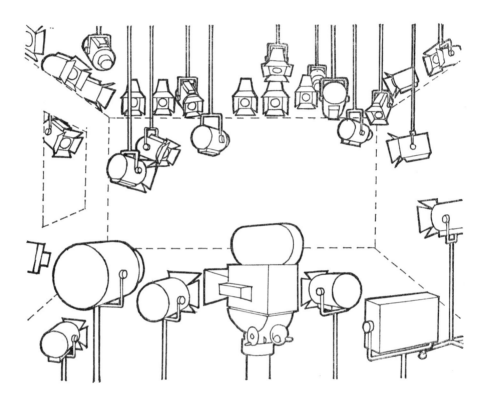

Studio lamps can be placed in virtually any position in relation to the subject they illuminate. They may be mounted on rails around the walls of the set, suspended from ceiling rails, placed on stands or even mounted on the camera itself. Sections of the set may be removed to aid camera movement or particular lighting arrangements. Additionally, the light may be controlled on the lamp by placing a filter over the front, shading by means of attachable barn doors, or a snoot.

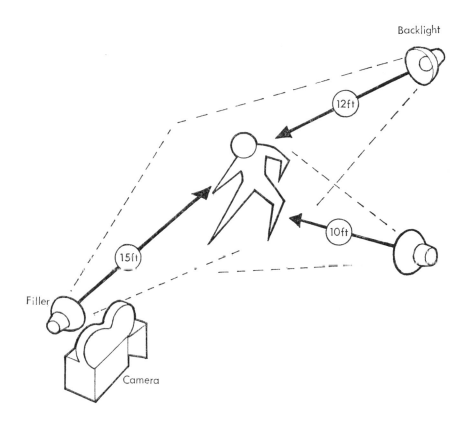

Basic functions of the three main lighting components in a hypothetical action shot—with relative distances. The key light placed at an angle to the camera viewpoint strikes the subject obliquely and models its contours. The fill light placed near to the camera viewpoint adjusts the ratio of highlights and shadow contrast by raising shadow illumination, without, however, creating hard shadows of its own. The backlight is an effect which may have many functions but usually enlivens the subject with small bright highlight areas, and improves separation from the background.

obstinate area of disturbing dark tone might be lifted by a spot directed at it, framed with barn doors to avoid any overspill. Flags or gobos can cut the background light at certain vertical points on the wall or corner to break up the background tonally or give freedom of action in the foreground. Banked spotlights from the rails above the set can provide much of this illumination.

For the actors themselves, a lensed light placed at a distance is much better to cover movement than an open pan from nearby. The spread may be nearly similar but variation in lighting intensity during movements is far less with the distant lamp with its near-parallel rays.

The actual lamp chosen to provide key light varies of course with the set up. If a brute might give a good key light for a scene in broad daylight, then for a candle-lit set up the key light could be a 500-W pup.

When several lamps are arranged so that one or two of them pick up an actor at closer range than the others, these are diffused or filtered to avoid overlighting him. But they must not be over-reduced. Naturally they should illuminate him more brightly than the other lamps if he is supposed to be nearer the light source in the scene.

LIGHTING AND ATMOSPHERE

The lighting of an indoor scene is modelled strictly according to the domestic lighting arrangement which has been planned by the art director to lend the room a certain characteristic atmosphere.

The atmosphere of the set is decided at the very beginning—the whole set adopts that nature in all its details.

The cameraman must try to create the same atmosphere as the art director is attempting to convey in his sets which in turn is called for in the script.

That atmosphere may be suggested, for example, by a single shadeless bulb hanging from the ceiling. The cameraman would try to create the effect of a mean room badly lit. The lighting would be harsh with shadows under the eyes, nose and chin and with everyone looking pretty dreary.

In another case an elegant living-room is seen pleasantly lit with various shaded lamps dotted about here and there. This demands a completely different character of lighting—perhaps of a mellow sort, softly diffused.

Let us take an example when the character of the lighting may actually have to be modified during the sequence.

A man returns to his apartment in the evening and as he opens the door he switches on the light. This is perhaps a ceiling light and the room is generally lit and very uninteresting. He goes into the bathroom,

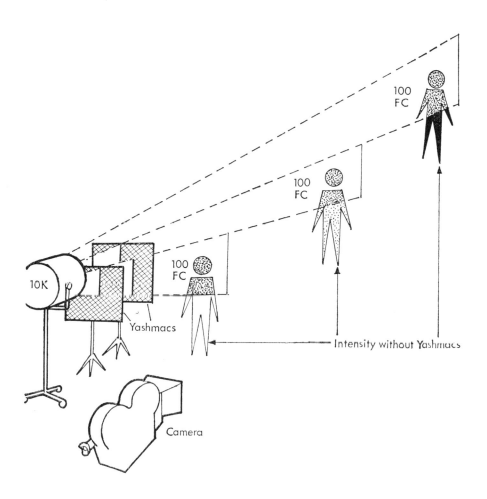

It is possible to keep a subject in the same kind of lighting at the same intensity with only one lamp plus windolite yashmacs (jelly on a stick) placed at different heights; for example, a lamp at 12 ft with one yashmac covering one-third, and another covering half the lamp vertically, could have the effect shown above.

and has a bath—he is expecting his fiancée later in the evening. When he is dressed he realizes she is due in twenty minutes. He looks around the room wondering how he can make it look more attractive. He turns on a couple of little lamps and switches off the overhead lights. The room immediately looks more romantic.

These details are valuable as they show the man's anticipation. A completely different atmosphere pervades the set before the girl arrives.

REAL LAMPS DO NOT LIGHT A ROOM

If a room were photographed using only those lights actually appearing in the picture the result on the screen would show two or three brightly lit shades and the rest of the set in total darkness.

Although they may be photographed, these lamps cannot themselves illuminate the room. Some additional lighting is always required. Sometimes quite elaborate studio lighting is needed to simulate the effect of just three lamps in a scene and make the result appear completely natural.

To gain realistic effects, studio lamps often have to be placed in the picture but hidden from view. The place chosen depends very much on the movement of the camera and actors. Sometimes it is almost impossible to conceal a light anywhere on the set. But most of the lighting for the majority of scenes comes from outside the camera's field of view.

A lamp appearing in the scene may be fitted with a photoflood in place of the normal lamp. This is considerably more powerful and would illuminate an actor sitting close by. If, however, he walked away he would soon disappear into darkness though it would not appear so to the human eye. It is necessary to correct for the peculiarities of photography in order to obtain a natural effect.

To gain a realistic rate of fall-off in light as he moves away, a second lamp is placed above and behind the first. This picks him up at a certain distance—in effect, gradually taking over from the first. One pool of light blends imperceptibly into the next, slightly diminishing in power. A further light might pick up the actor as he moves farther still into the room, again less brightly, so that as he walks away he gradually passes into semi-shadow. This light also appears to be coming from the same practical lamp which is motivating the effect.

The second and third lamps are angled in such a way that they carry brightness to certain points in the set where they cannot interfere with other lighting. A series of such lights could be used to cover the movements of an actor about the set so that he would be correctly lit at all times—and if desired, appear to be lit by this one practical lamp.

When photofloods are used inside conventional fittings which appear in the scene, it is important to choose a suitable shade. It should be diffused enough for the bulb not to be visible through the shade yet not so dense that the effect of the photoflood is cancelled out. The shade should be the right colour and texture of cloth, too. Diffusing material can often be placed inside a lampshade to cut down the light. This would still allow the full brightness of light to emerge from under the lampshade. Even so, the fall-off from any such light is tremendous. Correct lighting with the subject at 2 ft 6 in. gives serious underexposure with the subject at 5 ft unless he is picked up by a cheated light which is apparently coming from the same source.

FILL-IN FOR SHADOWS GENERALLY

Areas which are in shadow appear very black when filmed in colour. Far more fill-in light should be used than for, say, a fast black and white film, which records detail even in the darkest corners.

Sometimes you may simply leave the black areas unfilled—for dramatic effect. Much of the art in lighting is knowing where to leave certain areas dark so that they accentuate the brightly lit parts of the scene.

TRICKS FOR HANDLING LIGHT

With the help of the chief electrician, the cameraman devises many kinds of trick to achieve the lighting he has in mind. He may want the light to cut off at a certain point in the picture. A carefully positioned shading device such as a gobo or a French flag could do this. The cut-off may be a straight line, an angle or an irregular shape according to the position of the shading device and its pattern. A particular light may need to be narrowly controlled with a snoot or barn doors or it may need to be spread by being bounced off a prepared reflecting surface. Or, it may have to be focused on a certain spot or spread to weaken the effect by adjustment of a spotlight focus control. Any devices used for lighting control must not interfere with the realistic effect of the light whereby subjects become more softly lit as they move away from a visible light source.

SEPARATING ACTOR AND BACKGROUND

In every case the lighting of a set must ensure that there is suffi-cient tonal relief between an actor and his background. If, for example, the actor is wearing a dark suit the background must be balanced

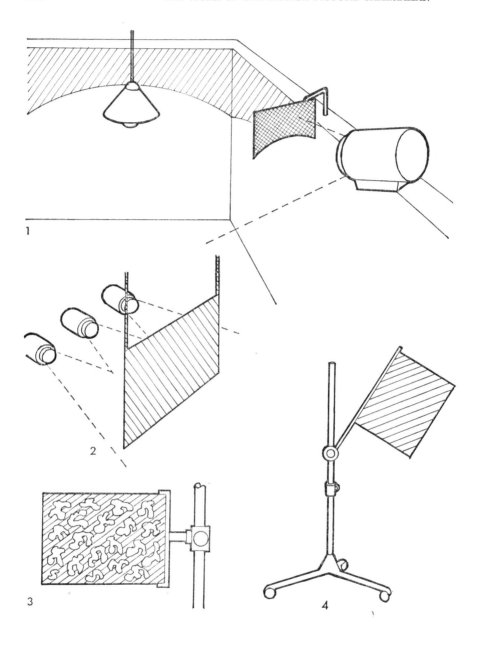

A shaped gobo 1, may be placed in front of a lamp on the lighting rail above the set to simulate a curved shaded area in the set supposedly caused by a practical lamp. A very large flag 2, may be suspended by ropes from the ceiling, cutting off a whole string of lights and shading a large part of the set. An ulcer 3, is a solid shader perforated by cut out shapes and designed to throw a dappled pattern in an area of the set. A small flag 4, is a rigid opaque shader on an adjustable Century stand.

accordingly. There must be enough tonal distinction between a woman in a white dress and a white wall in the set. Using lights, the relative densities could be modified so that her dress appeared lighter than the background. Alternatively it could appear slightly grey compared with the wall. This wall and dress lit without bias toward one or the other would give a flat overall effect. The same applies to the face.

This problem becomes even more acute when filming a moving actor. Furniture and other objects that lend variety to the background produce sudden changes of tonal scale as the camera follows the actor past them. Constant effort is needed whenever the actors move to keep them separate from the background in terms of light and shade. Moreover, the lighting must always appear natural—as if resulting from the lamps in the scene rather than lamps in the studio.

Now suppose there were only one main light in the room. If the subject were a Negress wearing a white dress and moving across the set in front of a large piece of dark furniture, such as a tallboy, the lighting could not be interfered with simply to solve the technical problem. She would be lit in more or less the same way throughout the shot. But when the camera follows her, it brings about a different balance of, or relationship between, the subject and background. If when she stood in front of the tallboy her face were almost the same tone as the background, she would be lit differently for the whole movement to separate them tonally. (For the one lamp that is supposed to be lighting the room there might be eight lamps working for it so that whatever position she walked into she would be separately lit but apparently from that one lamp.)

BACKGROUND CONTROL

Some other lamps or perhaps some of the same set cover the background, again as if lit by the domestic lamp. Here, however, backgrounds are fixed properties delineated in many cases by hard straight edges, so it is nearly always possible to flag or gobo the light off certain specific areas. The light may cover an actor in the normal way but be cut off down the edge of a door or piece of furniture behind, thus altering the relative brightness of various parts of the set. This lamp could be lighting both subject and background. There is no division of light on the actor where the lights change over—he goes straight through the sharp edge into the light from another lamp.

Good lighting often means a subtle interplay of many different devices, yet the result must always be logical and believable or the illusion of the film will not be sustained with conviction.

SHADOW AND MOVEMENT

An area of darkness can deliberately be introduced between two lamps. As long as the actor is well lit at the place where he stops moving after passing through shadow *en route* it is quite acceptable. It is quite pleasing for people to pass through light and shade as they move about the set. In fact, if they are seen in the same degree of light all the time, the scene has a dull, uninteresting flatness. As a pretty girl moves around the set, the modulation from light to shade adds to her attraction. When she stops she may be lit to look her most glamorous—but she can also look attractive in silhouette. Naturally, this also depends on the scene. If the expression on an actress' face is to be seen she must be in light— otherwise, she can be in shadow, perhaps to enhance the dramatic effect. Such ideas must be discussed in detail with the director beforehand and the actors should know, or at least it is often very good for them to know, that they are in shadow at a certain moment, and the reason why. It is always as well to let an actor know, particularly an important one, exactly what you are trying to do.

CONTINUITY OF ROOM LIGHTING

Nowadays one never looks at a set from one position only. It must be considered from the point of view of the action going on within it, from different angles on that action, and from the viewpoint of an actor walking through the set—his own viewpoint. So the camera is almost never stationary—though this depends upon the approach to the scene the director wants to make. Usually the camera is highly mobile during the scene.

The lighting in a room is consistent in respect of actual lamp positions. Light on a wall from a candle or lamp on a table remains there all the time, though from some angles it is quite insignificant. It may be close or far away, sharp or out of focus, but nevertheless, it still remains there.

Unfortunately, when the camera position is changed it is often necessary to alter the lights in order to convey the original effect.

If a certain wall were lit for the background of one shot, a change of camera position to the opposite corner could give a totally different effect. So some subtle alterations are made to the lighting so that it is compatible with the new angle, although seemingly lit by the same room lights. The cameraman tries to avoid extra movement and the additional work that it entails, but if he moves from one angle to another he invariably has to change the lighting. If he makes a 90° cut from one shot to another he needs to make changes, but if he moves the camera

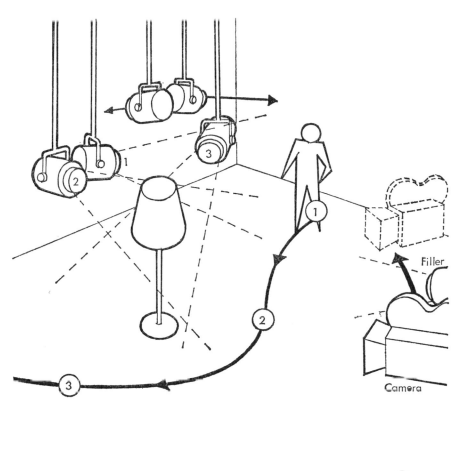

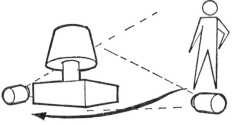

Possible basic lighting arrangement for a subject moving past a standard lamp at a distance of 6–8 ft allowing camera movement between the points shown. 1, 2 and 3 are slung from a bridge or rails above the set. Other lamps are provided for background illumination and a filler light is positioned close to the camera. With low position lighting for a table lamp lighting effect (*below*) as an alternative to the above, lamps may be hidden behind the table, etc., and placed on the floor.

through this arc in a tracking shot he has to make the best of it without changes.

Positioning Indoor Lights

With large interiors a high intensity of light may be needed in order to get sufficient depth of field. When lighting difficult interiors lights may have to be concealed in many places in front of the camera. Sometimes photofloods are substituted for the usual lamps in practicals but they must not be too bright. They may have to be frontally diffused.

In a long corridor the camera does not see the whole ceiling. The ceiling may only enter the picture area at a distance of 30 or 40 ft from the camera. Some of the lights can hug the ceiling just short of the viewing angle and provide a large amount of light deep in the scene. Lights can often be tucked behind odd corners and in doorways at the far end of the interior.

When designing a studio set, an art director might leave positions for the lights, or he might make it just as difficult to light as a real place.

The director of photography today has a very wide variety of lamps to choose from. They have been evolved through the requirements of cameramen over many years. But even with all these lamps he still finds it necessary to use pieces of plywood and tin, and clip-on diffusers to make a lamp do what he wants it to do.

Lighting is a very absorbing problem and constantly demands a great amount of improvisation.

The Harmful Effect of Multiple Shadows

If a subject is lit with six separate undiffused lamps, six distinct shadows are formed as the lamps can never be in exactly the same position as one another. The difference may be very small, but even so this effect destroys clarity and definition in the picture. Strictly speaking, one light is best for portraiture as it gives a single "clean" shadow yet decisive modelling to the contours of a face.

As the sun throws only one set of shadows we do not associate strong multiple shadows with natural lighting. When natural sunlight effects are imitated in the studio the single-shadow rule must always apply. This is basic.

Sunlight (or a single lamp in place of the sun) lends a feeling of roundness to a curved surface such as a pillar and hence an impression of solidity. Multiple lights destroy this roundness—the pillar becomes flat and the solidity is lost.

Suppose the pillar were of the fluted variety. The effect of the flutes would be very indistinct if hit by half a dozen different beams

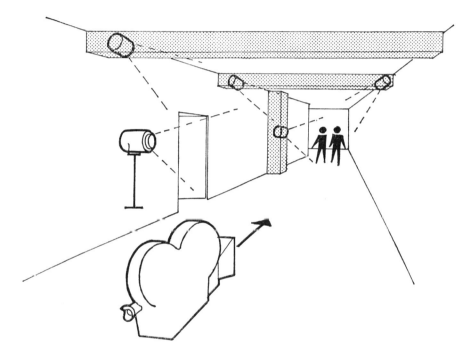

When the camera tracks along a corridor, illumination for the whole length may be provided by lamps hidden behind beams over the corridor or any convenient abutment with, perhaps, an additional effect lamp throwing light through an open door. Corridor beams may be included in the picture.

of light. Shadows would multiply so that if, say, six flutes were visible from a given angle and lit by six lamps, the muddle of thirty-six separate shadows would obliterate the shape of the fluting altogether. Also, the numerous shadows cause a loss of definition generally.

Definition is the visual shape of an object—not the sharpness. However sharp the camera lens is, multiple shadows give poor definition.

Multiple shadows can be avoided in the first place by using a simple lighting set up where only such a set up is called for. Starting from this premise it is plain that each further light added will add a separate shadow. This can be controlled, for example by diffusion or by the application of barn doors, gobos, flags and similar devices, before adding further lights. Otherwise it is possible to find yourself with a set of multiple shadows and no clear idea which lamps are the culprits, nor how to remedy the fault without throwing the whole lighting off balance. Because lighting is built up gradually, with lights in ratio with one another, if one needs alteration those based on it may also. These shadows can be avoided only by keeping a constant watch for them and correcting them as they appear. Prevention is better than cure and, with experience, they can be defeated even before switching on a light.

AVOIDING REFLECTIONS

Bright reflections in glass windows, mirror, bookcase, picture glass and similar surfaces are a distraction to the audience.

Usually the first thought to remedy unwanted reflections in a scene is to move the offending lamps. In certain situations this, indeed, may be the only way out of the problem and it may be straightforward for one lamp in the set to take over the duties of another. However, it is sometimes rather a fussy business and may lead to further complications in a completed set-up. Some simple expedient should be looked for wherever possible.

A bookcase with each of its six glass panes reflecting a light could be re-angled very slightly. Half an inch out of line would never show on the screen but could remove the reflections.

With window reflections it might be simpler to take a pane out but obviously that would not be done with an antique bureau. Windows in the set are normally held by a wooden flange rather than putty for this reason. The flange can be quickly taken out.

A tracking camera often picks up a series of reflections. But again one method or another can cure it, such as twisting the object, removing the glass or using some non-halation spray. This anti-flare treatment lessens the shine on a piece of chromium, for example, and subdues reflections without killing them altogether.

A glass of water may be treated with anti-flare on the outside, or the light may be flagged off at that particular point.

A sequin dress must look bright but not create an halation effect on the film. It is the angle of the lamp which governs this rather than its proximity to the subject.

Spectacle wearers should not be lit so that half a dozen lamp reflections are seen in the spectacles. But sometimes it is pleasant to see a point of light that livens them up. Where this effect is definitely ruled out ask the actor not to raise his head too much during the take. On some occasions it is possible to use spectacles without lenses. Where a character wears thick pebble glasses it is perhaps appropriate to accentuate this with highlight effects.

STEPPING UP LIGHTING POWER

Normally a scene is lit to a brightness level which takes into account the depth of field that will be needed for all shots involved. But for reasons technical or aesthetic, the director may suddenly ask for more depth even though he wants to retain the existing lighting set-up and mood. Because many cameramen (rightly) work with the minimum lighting output necessary for any particular scene, this means a step up in power.

To add to the power you replace the existing lamps with more powerful ones—a lamp cannot be made more powerful by adding another. Two lamps produce lighting which is quite different from one light. Besides, there is then no room on the lighting rail for another fitting.

The same exposure characteristic must be maintained throughout a scene when shooting, even if you have to double the lighting power in some shots for greater depth.

Suppose you are shooting a scene using a basic $f3.5$ (T4) setting which in terms of colour work (Eastmancolor Negative 5254) may mean that you have been shooting at, say, 200-ft candles with 2-kW lamps as your basic light. Now the director wants a door 15 ft from the camera in sharp focus as well as the actor who cannot be more than 5 or 6 ft from the camera. In this case, depending on the focal length of the lens in use, you may need to stop down to $f8$ or $f11$ for that much depth. Possibly 10-kW lamps would be necessary or even brutes, to raise the key to the required level. They could be brought in for this one shot and removed again afterwards although this would take a lot of time.

Reasons for working with lights of lower power for normal shooting are that it is simpler, means less heavy equipment need be moved about and consumes less electricity and is therefore more economical on all counts. But more important, you avoid too much depth of field for the average shot where you certainly do not need it, and perhaps para-mount, the actors do not have to work under the terrific strain that heat and light causes. Lighting that gives a working aperture of $f3·5–f4·5$ is usually quite adequate.

A more extreme case would be if you had to change from a pup (175-W) to a 10-K light. Extra depth would demand a change to a lamp ten times more powerful. Here the spread of light is much greater so the powerful light would have to be funnelled down. But for every necessity that you see in a scene you should have the ideal lamp for doing it, if possible.

If the director calls, for some reason quite out of the ordinary, for a jump from a pup to a brute, then it would be necessary to rethink and relight the set, although he wants exactly the same mood but with greater depth. The characteristics of these big lights are quite different from the small ones and lighting would have to be reworked bearing these differences in mind in order to arrive at the same result.

On a thirty-light set-up where more depth was needed the main light source could well be replaced with an arc light (plus colour correction filter). For one particular shot five or six very powerful lamps might be brought on to substitute the thirty small lights pre-viously in use—where, for example, the director thought some back-ground detail too insistent.

Stepping Down Lighting—Using Few Lamps

A cameraman need not step down the lighting from the existing intensity to achieve a shallow depth of field. He could use the shutter control on the camera to vary the exposure time. With cameras not equipped with variable shutter a neutral density filter may be employed.

Every lamp should be used for a definite purpose. Every extra light is a menace, because it gives another shadow which means another problem to avoid the hideous effects of multiple shadows. It is very pleasant if you have enough light with only two or three lamps. It is wonderful to use just one lamp and it can be done, but it is rarely sufficient. One lamp on a portrait is perfect with perhaps a little reflected light for filling in.

Effect of Time Passing—With Lighting

A finished sequence may take ten minutes to run through on the screen. But during that ten minutes, for the purposes of the story, the sequence might start in broad daylight and end with dusk falling. In reality this may be impossible within so short a space of time. But the ten minutes of screen time does not represent real time, and may with cuts and other devices quite reasonably represent the hours in the story. The changing light must be put across gradually and with some subtlety by the cameraman. After ten minutes the actor may draw the curtain and put on a light perhaps indicating that something is going to happen immediately afterwards and establishing the onset of nightfall.

LIGHTING EXPOSURE AND CONTRAST

Once he embarks on lighting a scene the cameraman works to a predetermined exposure, one that he thinks suitable for various factors indicated in the script. This standard working aperture which might range between *f*2 and *f*8 takes account of any changes in exposure that may take place in the scene, movement of actors, depth of field required and other factors indicated by the script.

In his mind's eye—and experience gives him one—and with the help of his pan-glass he can see what effect this lighting is going to have on the film. This is not necessarily how the set appears. To the uninitiated the set seems a blaze of light. But this is of course relative to the exposure given and the difference in the sensitivity of the photographic emulsion in comparison with that of the human eye and the increase in contrast of the photographic image.

Uses of a meter

Though a cameraman may be accustomed to using a meter all the time he is working, he must not let the meter light the set. His judgment and artistry must achieve it. After all, there are many times when a character may move into a shadow area where no reading is possible. This is done for a particular effect, and the meter is hardly the arbiter in these circumstances.

All present-day film processing is under the strictest time control. A cameraman bases his judgment on this purely mechanical known quantity. With the meter he can make sure that he keeps within the standards he has set himself. It is an aid to consistency.

Exposure and contrast-factors involved

The correct exposure on an indoor set cannot be determined by taking a general reflected light reading, pointing the meter in the shooting direction. In the studio, lamps would inevitably shine onto the cell with its relatively wide angle of acceptance. The more reliable method is to take an incident light reading from the light source itself and base the lighting level upon that. Alternatively a spot meter can be very useful for reflected readings.

A character placed on a chair in a certain position under a lamp might be the brightest part of a scene for a particular shot. That part appears at a certain brightness, determined by the chosen stop. The rest of the set is balanced with this, so that the cameraman knows exactly how bright any part of the set will be.

The knowledge of how bright certain parts of the scene may be takes into account, among other things, the colour of the set. Dark clothes or objects may have to be pulled away from dark backgrounds by lighting. There may be many cases where contrast must be controlled locally around the set, so that foregrounds and backgrounds blend or separate as the script may require.

Working method with a meter

When lighting the set an incident reading is taken of a given light from the position of the artist. This is usually the key light and it decides the aperture to be set on the lens. The rest is done as we noted before by judgment, but it is sometimes a help to look through a neutral density viewing glass to determine contrast, or to use the old trick of half closing the eyes—a method whereby shadow areas become much more pronounced and the scene is reduced to bold areas of light and shade. Balancing for dark objects is then done so that everything is rendered in realistic tone values. There is a particular danger that colours may be mistaken for tones. The cameraman must have some idea how certain colours are rendered differently on the emulsion of colour film. It may not be easy to distinguish between them, and lighting can be used to make up for this deficiency.

Usually the exposure meter is calibrated in foot-candles. There are about half a dozen popular models to choose from. When working out the exposure the cameraman knows the speed of the film, and if it is necessary to shoot the scene at, say, $f4 \cdot 5$ to obtain enough depth. From this he may decide that he needs 250 foot-candles and that the key light is roughly this. Fill in lights will not greatly influence this—exposure in them may be only 50 foot-candles or less.

The lighting is done entirely by the director of photography and no one checks his exposure readings. All setting of lights is done by the electricians. Among other personnel under the director of photography are the stand-by chippie, painter and plasterer. They are there all the time to make lightning alterations to the set and perhaps remove, replace or repaint certain parts which may be necessary for changes in the lighting plan.

Remembering lighting set-ups

It frequently happens when shooting large productions that, either for budget reasons, or because of the absence of an actor, a scene shot today cannot be continued for two or three weeks. It is advisable to ask the gaffer (chief electrician) if he will try to memorize the lighting involved so that it is easier to reconstruct it when needed. This is only a safeguard—as it is chiefly the cameraman's job to remember, though with a complex set up the gaffer may have a better idea of the number and type of lamps involved rather than their position.

Strangely enough a cameraman does remember exactly where he has put the lights, and he can recall this even over a period of two or three weeks. Certain difficulties arise when lighting a scene and these become imprinted in his mind, especially if he knows he will return to them. Should a scene he has shot, say, in his last film, have been destroyed or lost he could relight and shoot the scene again to tie up with the rest of the film.

Contrast

The lighting ratio suggested by a film manufacturer for any particular film is a purely theoretical figure. It is based on average results under laboratory conditions. No cameraman working on average results is going to produce anything very exciting. The kind of effect he may wish to secure will often mean taking liberties with the film material.

Suppose the basic working aperture has been determined by the size of the set and the number and size of lights available and the figure $f4.5$ arrived at. Some parts of the scene may go down to $f1$ and the top light be fully exposed at $f4.5$. All grades of illumination between the top light and the darkest part of the set are somewhere between these two stops. Underexposed parts will still be visible when shooting at $f4.5$ and the top exposure will not be too high. This is worked out in accordance with the film being used and the flexibility of operation varies with film.

With monochrome materials there is a choice of emulsion speed and the contrast range varies accordingly. When using different materials the contrast must be compensated with the lighting. Generally a cameraman uses material of only one type for one production—or perhaps two types, one each for exteriors and interiors.

A fast black and white emulsion would be used also at a much lower stop than usual, which compensates largely for the difference in contrast. In this instance the material might have been chosen originally because of a need for deep focus in a particular part of the film. With a fast film, for deep focus, you may be working at $f8$ or an even smaller aperture. The film is so fast that it needs very little light.

With colour film, conditions are entirely different. Only one speed is widely available so you are dealing with a fixed quantity. Effects are obtained not by choice of material but by control of lighting exposure and such devices as filters and screens which also change the colour. In a moonlight scene, for example, you underexpose and filter so that you pass from a cold outdoor light to a warm indoor one. In colour you are constantly working with colour filters. Colour film is rather more contrasty than the equivalent black and white.

Actually, the mixing of colour "light-source" effects does not always look too happy in a scene. It can be confusing to have some blue light creeping into a room which is suddenly lit by warm light inside. In a real scene moonlight would not show, anyway, once this light had been switched on. So an electrician should dim, cover or switch off the moonlight as the warm light is switched on.

ATTITUDES TO LIGHTING

In making a film it is the prime concern of the director, the cameraman, art director and everyone concerned to capture, and somehow improve on, the atmosphere that the scriptwriter had in mind. For the cameraman it is a question of combining lighting and camera work in the most suitable and interesting way.

Value of lighting

Although it is an ideal worth working toward, one could hardly expect to improve on the lighting, seen in paintings, perfected by those painters of the past who excelled in this direction. It is impossible to outdo them for this kind of lighting. But the problem with motion pictures is that the cameraman has to do so many set-ups each day that he is inclined to fall into constant repetition. He tends to use a basic key lighting so that he can see facial expressions all the time. In the long run this becomes monotonous. If he has the chance to work on the type of picture where artistic effect is the main concern, he has an opportunity to work out the type of lighting that will give mood and atmosphere. Sometimes the director will leave the field wide open to the cameraman and invite him to take his time. He can then do his very best within the context of the script. Some directors recognize the possibilities of good lighting and its value to the film. Others do not. These directors might simply think in terms of dialogue and funny gags. It is satisfying for a cameraman to work with a director who appreciates lighting.

"Style" in lighting and camera work

Cameramen do develop recognizable styles of their own. Some cameramen have made a name by producing very good exterior camera work. They may have shot a number of Westerns, for example, with intensive use of certain filters. Their work may be instantly recognizable where these techniques are used in a particular way. But "style" as such, can become too much a preoccupation. And it is probably better to try to avoid this kind of conscious or perhaps self-conscious method. It is more advisable to aim at lighting a film according to the subject and the ideas that are to be put over. The lighting of one film is then in a completely different vein from that of another. The very fact that events are supposed to take place in one part of the world or another should be a primary influence in the lighting, thus giving an atmosphere of its own.

There are great dangers if a cameraman should have what he considers a definitive style. As with a painter, the lighting must be imaginative but in the cameraman's case not in the same style each time.

6

Lighting for Situations and Effects

In many situations lighting may be used to emphasize the ideas the cameraman tries to convey with the camera. In a scene where one man is intended to dominate another, lighting on the dominant personality might emphasize the special characteristics of his face— a face made up or selected in the first place for its expressive potential. With suitable lighting, the more grizzly aspect of a face may be brought out. Lines may be accentuated by placing the key light well above or below the level of his face. A more flat and less severe lighting may make a man's character appear weaker.

Lighting tricks such as these must be done with subtlety and in such a way that the lighting is still acceptable. Dramatic lighting cannot suddenly be injected into the middle of a sequence—this could look quite wrong and the audience would be very aware of the incongruity.

A gradual change in the lighting during a scene will not be noticed. It can be most useful where, for example, you want a sort of gradual Jekyll/Hyde transformation in a character. The person may appear perfectly normal at the outset and without any change of camera position or cut in action, he may have to change into a loathsome creature—all without jarring effect or indication of light juggling. The person himself must appear to change rather than the set. If this were to be shot (in black and white, to simplify the example) starting in normal lighting, lamps could be arranged for the other end of the scene where the light comes from extreme angles and makes the character appear grotesque. During the actual shot, dimmers could be used to effect a gradual transfer from one set of lights to the other.

A more complex but extremely potent way of indicating such a change is to filter a particular lamp so that it brings out certain coloured

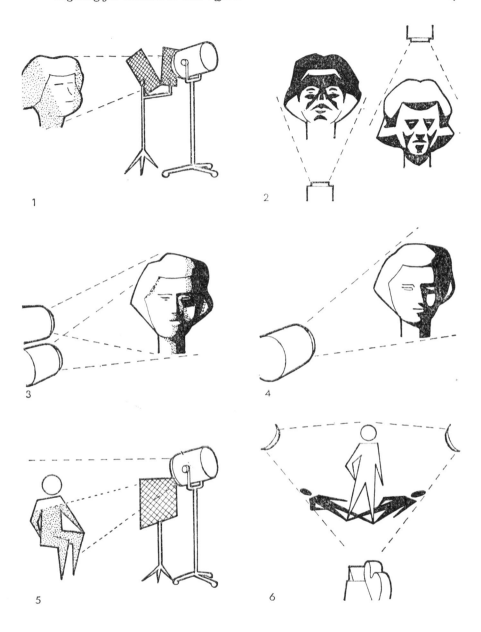

Light manipulation: 1, a rotund face may be "narrowed" by shading with gauzes positioned in the light beam. 2, Lights directly beneath and above the face produce striking modelling effects. 3, Multiple lights give confusing multiple shadows and may destroy definition in the picture whereas 4, a single set of shadows gives clearly defined modelling. 5, Lower or less important part of the subject may draw too much attention to itself, a gauze may reduce the light intensity at that point and redirect attention to the face. 6, Cross-lighting gives opposing shadows.

shading on the actor's face. This shading must be designed to emphasize different aspects of the face and the exact choice of colouring and matching filter is thought out beforehand. Again, using a dimmer on this particular lamp the change would be brought about gradually.

In another example, a girl seen through the eyes of a hero may perhaps have not been particularly noticeable to him at the beginning of the scene. Later, she grows on him and he begins to see her as someone new and very attractive. The lighting can be modified to shape out the process of thought in the man's mind when the girl changes from an anybody to somebody.

When lighting a girl to make her look as attractive as possible, every artifice has to be used. Even a catchlight in the hair is not out of date. The cameraman makes his own assessment of the girl's face and decides on the best kind of lighting. Then he tries a few lights in different positions and picks the most attractive arrangements.

When a young man meets a girl and becomes enamoured, the lighting must put this over to the audience. It is even possible, subject to the script, to show an obvious change of light—like a fairy-tale—from the man's viewpoint. Here the cameraman has to be a portraitist as well as a cinematographer. It would be much more subtle to vary the lighting than make the girl move into a more romantic light in the next room. Another method is to arrange soft lighting in the foreground, so that at some point in the action the actress comes forward to a close-up position where the lighting is most favourable. Her face may fill the screen and she appears most beautiful.

Diffusion Screens and Their Uses

To soften the appearance of a woman's face a diffused light can be used—a diffused spotlight rather than a hard spotlight. At close range it is normal to use a slight diffusing screen over the camera lens. At very close range where lines in the face and even pores of the skin are clearly visible, a heavy diffusing screen may be used.

Diffusing screens are supplied in sets graded A, B, C or 1, 2, 3 according to the amount of diffusion they give. The usual type have a pattern or rings in the glass. Sometimes a gauze may be used. A piece of chiffon or nylon stocking can be mounted on a piece of cardboard and placed in front of the lens.

Focus is determined by a tape measure so the question of focusing a diffused image through a lens need not arise. A glass type diffusing screen does not require any compensating change in exposure, whereas a slight change may be needed with a gauze. Fairly wide working apertures should be used with clear-centre discs as stopping down means that only the central area of the lens is being used and then only the

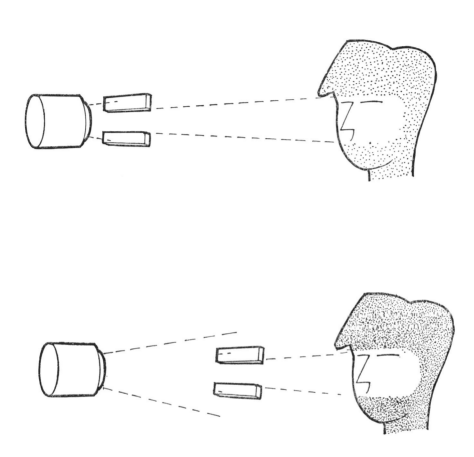

To produce shadow effects at a particular point in the action charlie bars (small laths) may be mounted close to the lamp or farther away, depending on the hardness of the effect required.

central or clear glass area of the screen. This would reduce diffusion or cancel it out altogether.

A gauze is frequently used when shooting in colour. It depends upon the type of diffusion required. A starred effect in the reflections and highlights may be pleasing in a certain scene. This can be achieved with a gauze though not with a glass diffuser. Gauze can give a very subtle diffusion. Some threads can be pulled out or a hole burnt in the centre so that only the outer part of the picture is diffused.

Glass screens marked OB have bevelled rings and are heavy diffusers. The OA type are lighter. But these are only made in certain sizes to fit certain lenses.

With larger lenses such as those used in 70-mm cinephotography it is often necessary to improvise. Larger glass screens are available— pieces of glass with an even diffusion all over, done not by bevelled rings but an ingredient in the glass itself. These are available in various strengths.

A diffuser is not used on a medium shot except for some special effect such as haze, or where the vision of a character is impaired, and the audience is supposed to see the scene as he does.

LIGHTING FACES—TONE VALUES

An actor who is required to move during a shot presents lighting problems peculiar to cinematography. When he remains in one position for any length of time he may be, and in fact should be, lit as carefully as a good studio portrait.

Two actors with differing complexions should take the same key of light if they are to be represented as different on the screen. Occasionally the actual difference may be greater than desired. On film, differences of tone may be attenuated. If they need to be "pulled together" a little the make-up artist can tone down or lighten the other.

At the beginning of a film, actors should be more or less related to one another tonally by the make-up artist. On occasions, they may have to bridge a considerable gap. One actor may look washed out and the other deeply tanned. Light may sometimes be used to gain this effect, or more usually, to add to it. It depends upon the story.

Lights could help out with the sort of contrast problem encountered where, for example, a Negro and a fair person are seen together looking out of a window. An additional lamp may raise the tone a little where in that particular position the Negro looks too black. In a more complex set-up a series of small lamps all round the set may be needed for one particular person.

When the average white person is overlit his skin appears bleached out. Lighting must be for skin texture. An overlit face has no texture and, in fact, tends to bounce the light back—a further lighting hazard. In certain circumstances, however, deliberate overlighting is permissible, as when a torch is shone into someone's face, temporarily blinding them. This is the exceptional case and has no bearing on general practice. Here the unpleasant side effects are accepted as natural.

MOISTURE AND PERSPIRATION EFFECTS

In the studio on a warm day when many lights are in use to cope with some special problem of focus depth, the natural outcome is that the actors perspire. Unwanted perspiration is a hazard to facial make-up and the make-up artists must be constantly on the alert, particularly where close-ups are involved. In more extreme temperatures an actor may sweat through his shirt, and a quick change is necessary—the spare shirt must be there.

In cold conditions where the actor is intended to sweat, water, glycerine or a mixture of these can be applied to his face. Glycerine is used wherever a moist subject must remain moist in appearance and would otherwise soon dry out under the heat of the lights. To reduce the effect of heat on a still life subject a sheet of glass can be placed in front of the light to absorb some of the heat, and the lamp only turned up to full power immediately before shooting.

LIGHT BALANCING FOR INTERIORS

When using real interiors during the daytime light must, almost unavoidably, be provided both by artificial means and the daylight coming through the window. Daylight alone is very rarely adequate for filming in such situations except for the isolated instance where the characters may be seen right next to the window and in very close view where the background is more or less excluded. Modern buildings with large plate-glass windows may provide a substantial amount of daylight, but it is always very directional and cannot, of course, be controlled. Control over lighting is of prime importance to the lighting cameraman, particularly where many scenes are required in any given location. He prefers to use lights for most situations and is constantly bringing them in to supplement the daylight.

The problem with using colour indoors is the widely differing characteristics of daylight and some artificial light sources in terms of colour temperature. When using arc lights with white flame carbons a WF Green filter is used to convert the light to approx. 5400 K. However, with small rooms (relatively small that is), where arc lights are impractical and incandescent light is used, an "85" filter must be placed over the window itself. This converts the daylight value from approx. 5400 K to that of incandescent light, i.e. 3200 K. This filter material is available in large rolls several feet wide and as much as 20 yds long. A complication that comes with using this is that any light you put inside is inclined to be reflected as bright spots in the gelatin sheet. Moreover, if it is windy outside the gelatin will blow about. In recent years a great improvement on the gelatin filter is the thick Perspex filter which does not crinkle or move in the wind, and this material can be obtained in neutral densities of 0·3–6 and 0·9 plus in combination with the "85" filter, and these are now in common use. These figures represent percentage densities of a solid black.

The negative used has a colour sensitivity range balanced for use with incandescent light 3200 K and requires an "85" filter over or behind the camera lens if it is used for normal outdoor shooting. This filter has the same effect as the material used over windows.

Lighting balance may be a matter of power as well as colour. Very large interiors demand arc illumination in any case and it is sometimes necessary to use as many as 30 arcs to obtain sufficient brilliance. In the film *Lawrence of Arabia*, an enormous building in Seville was used, which had a range of rooms, corridors and courtyards. Brilliant sunshine outside had to be balanced with the very shaded interior during long tracking shots through the doorways.

The limitation on arcs in small rooms is not their power, which can always be reduced by diffusion, but the smoke and heat which always comes from their carbons. This will soon fill a small space and become objectionable.

Shooting Into a Room From Outdoors

If, in a studio set up, a scene inside a room is taken through a window with someone outside eavesdropping, lighting the interior and "exterior" is comparatively easy. Studio lights may be arranged to provide correct balance of light between the two parts of the set.

This balance can suit the scene exactly. Details may be visible in both parts, or one may predominate. Such adjustments are hardly an obstacle where a cameraman has these facilities at his disposal.

In a real location the brilliance of sunlight or even daylight makes this balance less easy to achieve. Sunlight must be combated by the strength of artificial lights without any appearance of overlighting. Moreover, the daylight not only dictates the artificial lighting for the rest of the set but it is subject to the usual fluctuations (i.e. passing clouds, etc.) which will upset the balance.

In terms of photographing, a room appears black to a person outside in the sun. If the window forms only a very small part of the scene the black appearance may in some cases remain. But in cases where the actor looks through the window and we share his view to some extent, the inside of the room must be seen. This is especially so if we go up to the window, for when we do this in real life we can nearly always see through even if the window is closed.

When working against daylight quite powerful lights are needed inside the room. There is, however, a danger of overlighting the interior. It must still appear rather darker than the outside scene, with visible but more shadowy details.

If you were standing outside in bright sunlight and suddenly looked through a door or window, the inside of the room would look very dark. Your eyes must grow accustomed to it. For the purposes of photography this adjustment must be made gradually. The cameraman moves toward the window and as he draws near makes a gradual change in exposure so that the audience can see inside the room as soon as the window occupies a significant part of the picture area. Obviously exposure changes of this nature alter the tone values and possibly the colour also, of the scene outside the window. One does not want to draw attention to this; so the degree of adjustment must be timed in the track to start at a point where this change would remain unnoticed.

The necessary compensation in exposure can be worked out on the diaphragm of the lens or alternatively using the shutter of the camera. A meter reading would give the two limits and the assistant cameraman can make the change as the camera moves in.

With this technique a balance of lighting is not so important because the change in exposure makes up for the difference in subject brightness. But there is a limit to what can be done. In practice, some artificial light is always necessary inside the room because too great a change in exposure is beyond the range of the shutter or the diaphragm.

If in a daytime shot, there was *supposed* to be no artificial light in the room and the window or door were open, the scene must be lit as if the light were coming through that window or door. From the outside the light looks rather flat, as it would in reality. But flat lighting is an evil one always tries to do away with in the average scene. Here it cannot be done away with but the flatness can be played down a little. With some modulation in the lighting, it could appear natural without being too flat. A few lights judiciously positioned inside the window would provide enough extra light and give the desired contrast increase.

SUNLIT INTERIORS WITH DRAWN CURTAINS

For a "sunlit" interior scene, lighting is positioned inside as well as outside the set. Light coming through the window and supposedly lighting the set is in fact heavily supplemented by "interior" lighting, suggesting the effect of daylight through the window.

If the net curtains are closed on arc "sunlight," the interior lighting may be not only dimmed but diffused. The character of the lighting has changed. Net curtains closed on an arc may cause excessive glare. As the curtains are drawn the arc would be dimmed not through a resistance (which would alter the colour temperature and, of course, intensity) but with a "dimmer shutter." This is a series of louvres on the lamp which can be turned to reduce the light intensity by degrees. Interior lamps might be diffused simultaneously using diffusing screens. These actions must be timed to coincide with the closing of the curtains or the procedure reversed for opening the curtains.

Excessive glare from net curtains closed in the path of an arc arises simply because the curtains are white. Often the curtains may be treated by a dipping process known as "Tec One" or "Tec Two." They are dipped in a diluted dye so that the white becomes pale grey. This method has been widely used for reducing the "hot" effect of a light striking pure-white materials and props.

The term "Tec" comes from Technicolor, the early system. It was soon found when working with the early colour process that white sheets, pillow cases, shirts, tablecloths and curtains all came out with too much glare.

The dipping is roughly divided into three categories, "Tec Three" being the darkest. White clothes, especially shirts, are often treated in this way.

Church Interiors—A Special Problem

The camera team may spend a very long time in a church covering only a single sequence. If the church has stained-glass windows and it is daytime the scene is shot as if these windows provide the light. In the early morning when the sun has risen the east window does indeed provide plenty of light. But often within an hour or two the sun is off the window and powerful lamps must be set up striking the window outside to simulate the effect for the remainder of the scene. In order to avoid the complication of reflections it is usual to light as though the principal source is the windows, plus, if there are candles burning *en masse* (as, for example, in a Roman Catholic church) an additional source from these. The candles are an inconsiderable source in themselves but they show up when included in the shot and it is essential to augment that effect with lamps or they will appear quite unrealistic in the general lighting scheme. The tiny flame shows up quite distinctly and must be accepted as a light source and lit accordingly.

As with all such schemes where false lighting is used to give

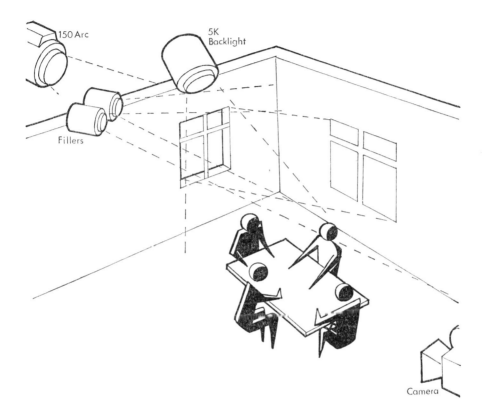

Indoor lighting (daytime). The "sunlight" through the window throwing a sunlit shape on the wall is provided by a 150-amp arc placed behind the set striking it from an angle depending on the latitude and time of day. A 5-K lamp on a rail above the set provides backlighting for the people at the table, and soft fill light for the sunlit wall comes from two lamps on a rail. The rear wall can be given soft, shadowed, lighting by frontally placed lamps.

realism, it must be carried through to the details. The lamps for this area should be filtered to give a warm glow and the correct amount of light must be used so that the candles appear as a genuine light source. The length of the candles must also be checked. Candles must be changed often in scenes which are supposed to take place within a few minutes of one another, so that they appear more or less the same length. If the scene is scanned with a certain lapse of time, the long candle must be replaced by one appropriately burnt down. The changes should be taken in hand by the property man, under the vigilant eye of the continuity girl.

The appropriate atmosphere for a church is rendered with shadowy areas, the warm glow from the candles, fairly dark walls and the windows showing up quite brightly. The coloured glass in a church window naturally causes a great reduction in light. Dark red glass, for example, acting like a red filter drops the brightness by a factor of 4 at least.

The principal difficulty with church interiors is undoubtedly to maintain consistency in the day's work. In a scene of two minutes screen time the sun may have moved right round from east to west. While the lamps outside provide the "sunlight" through the east window, it may be necessary to put a neutral density filter over the west or south windows to reduce the effect of the real sunlight which has in the meantime moved round. These filters can be prepared in sheet form made up in frames and mounted outside the windows. The filter might be 25 per cent, 50 per cent or 75 per cent neutral density, reducing the light to the correct level according to the angle of the sun.

The churches that are normally used by film companies are functioning, not disused ones, and permission has to be obtained to use them. Whether or not that permission is forthcoming depends on the story of the film and the opinion of it that the vicar or priest has formed. People involved must move about carefully and quietly and show respect for the place they are working in. Just outside there are probably generators and a catering wagon to feed the crew. All this must be done discreetly. The team may have to withdraw from the church for special services or weddings. Normally the company are notified that they can work between certain specified hours. The production manager sees to it that something is given to the church funds.

The inside of a cathedral is a pretty monumental lighting job. With colour especially, a tremendous amount of light is needed. When a small corner of a church is used, seeing perhaps 20 ft up a pillar quite a large quantity of light is essential, even for that. If anything much higher were needed it could be done with a matt shot with the top half painted in.

If the church scene was a long and important sequence the building

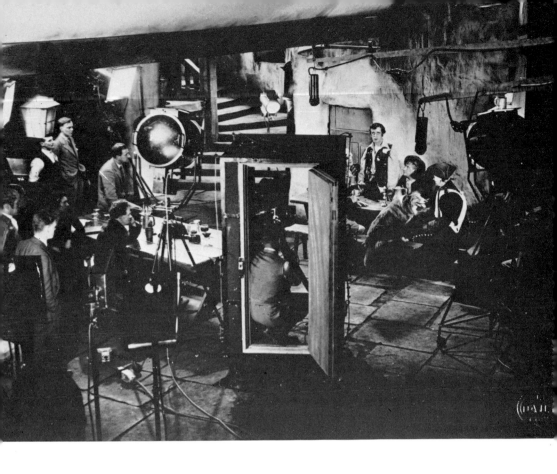

Early Talkie, *Loves of Robert Burns* (1930) showing camera and operator in an airtight sound-proof booth. Later on, the camera was blimped and the operator could breathe again. Eventually cameras were silenced and self-blimped but even today sound men still grumble about camera noise at close range.

Page 138 *Treasure Island* (1950—Walt Disney)
Technicolor three-strip camera on Academy crane
under low roof in captain's cabin set.

(Above) *Caesar and Cleopatra* (1944—Rank) Egyptian
location with plaster sphinx and improvised wind
machines for making a sand storm.

(Right) Adjusting the setting of the light on a brute.

Page 140 (Top) *Lawrence of Arabia*. Watering the
desert prior to a cavalry charge; the camera, on a
crane, has a sunshade. (Bottom) Camels, late
afternoon, with long shadows.

Page 141 *Nicholas and Alexandra*. Lining up Jack
and Janet Suzman. (Bottom) Franklin Schaffner
directing Janet and Roderic Noble.

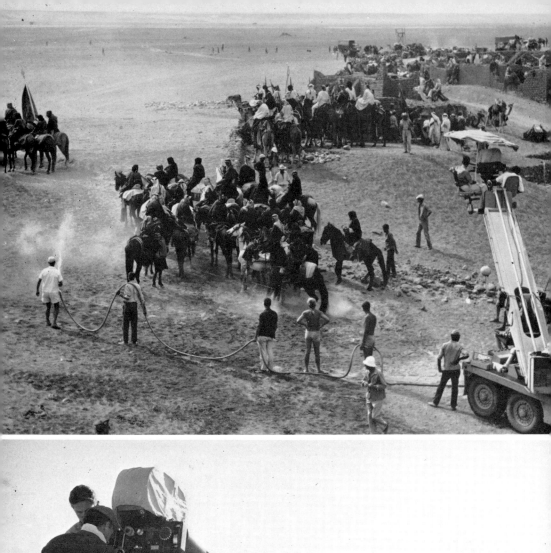

(Top) *Ryan's Daughter*. Storm sequence; camera chined down to rocks, shooting through clear screen. (Left) Revolving screen.

Page 143 (Top) *Ryan's Daughter*. Seven brutes used on dull day to increase daylight exposure. (Bottom) Discussing a tracking shot across rocks.

(Top) *Ryan's Daughter*. Tracking shot on the beach showing the method of extending the camera out from the crane to avoid track marks in the sand in a shot of Robert Mitchum and Sarah Miles. (Left) Pointing the direction for Sarah Miles to walk, which had to be done correctly at the first attempt to avoid marking the virgin sand.

could be constructed in the studio. There perspective can be faked and a painted background used for half of it. This would simplify the lighting considerably. If filming is to take a week it would probably be impractical to use a real church. One cannot expect to "take over" a church every day for a week.

The generators should be at some distance from the church, and with baffles to deaden the sound as much as possible. These baffles usually take the form of a wooden framework with heavy felt on both sides. Large cables from the generators may have to cross a road at some point so bevelled boards are placed over them. Traffic approaching them slows down and bumps over the boards which protect both cable and tyres from impact. Here police co-operation is obligatory.

STUDIO "DAYTIME" INTERIORS

In the studio, where an interior scene must include the effect of sunlight streaming through the window, incandescent light may form the primary source for general illumination. But only an arc light is strong and sharp enough to dominate this set-up with incisive shadows for the full effect of sunlight. This arc would be used with a gel to match it to the general lighting. Colour values must be identical where the room is supposed to be lit by daylight.

Colour film nowadays provides for a reasonable amount of exposure latitude, and it is possible to light so that the outside looks correct and the inside a little darker. But there are limitations to the film latitude and these are best learned through practice. Studio lights are designed to give a constant 3200 K, and the electrician must watch that the voltage is maintained at the correct level. If too many lamps are used from one generator their colour tends toward yellow with light loss. To maintain correct colour, a colour temperature meter is sometimes necessary. Ageing lamps do not change much in colour temperature but simply become dim. A reading from quite an old "bubble" will reveal almost the same Kelvin value although its output is less.

INDOOR SCENE IN DAYLIGHT

Interior lighting in broad daylight is usually diffused. But if someone is standing at the window looking out, there is a mixture of direct sunlight on their face and diffused light reflected from the immediate surroundings. If they look through curtains, the light is rather diffused by the net or lace.

Where sunlight through the window throws a pattern on the floor nearby, the remainder of the light is reflected—soft light from the window giving soft shadows. This is *directional*, soft light coming from the window as distinct from the general soft lighting of a night interior lit by two or three shaded lamps.

Light in the scene apparently all coming from the window might be indicated by, say, one powerful arc lamp directed through the window. But that in itself does not light the room. Other lamps must be used inside the room yet give the impression that all the light is coming from the window.

The lighting of this scene must take into account the fact that the whole room is not seen all the time. There might be one or two long shots where the window and a large part of the room are seen together. But the remaining shots are possibly close-ups with the window in the background, or the other way round, shooting away from the window. These close shots allow the lamps to be moved to the best advantage of each shot provided the lighting appears unaltered on the film. Here the lighting must, of course, always be logical in the circumstances of the scene.

When a room is in long shot with a window to the left, the face of a person standing in the room is lit from the window side. If the camera moves in front of the window facing toward the person the light on his face is flat—not from the side.

In the long shot the lighting might appear to be all from one side yet in the close up with the camera backing onto the window the lighting is frontal.

If the camera faces the window, the subject becomes backlit. In this event a soft reflective light must be put on the face, otherwise it is in silhouette.

All these degrees of modulation in light depend on the mood of the scene and whether it is supposed to be broad sunlight outside or a dull winter's day.

Lighting for colour film creates additional problems. Late afternoon sunlight or sunset requires gelatine filters over the lamps, giving an orange or pinkish effect. With black and white only degrees of lighting strength are important.

A problem of contrast arises when shooting a brightly lit view seen through a window. If the set is a real house and it is a real scene outside, the daylight becomes the key light and enough light must be provided to balance with the daylight.

A large proportion of such scenes are shot in the studio. Here the view through the window may be provided by a painted backing or back projection, or a photographic background. In each case interior lighting must be appropriately balanced, that is, it must be sufficient to see any action in the room but give the appearance of a natural interior with daylight outside, i.e. the indoor lighting is less bright in proportion.

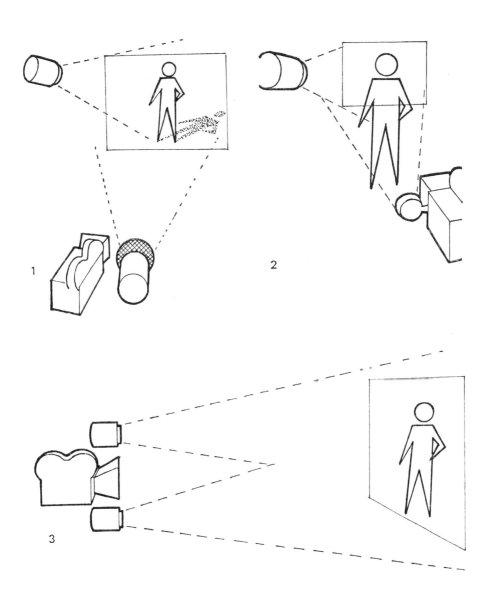

Fill lights: 1, Single shadow, one light plus diffused fill lamp near camera position. 2, For close ups the fill light may be a small basher lamp on the camera itself. 3, For longer shots there may be one lamp either side of the camera, and close to it, or one under and one over, i.e. in line with the camera.

If the main intention is to focus the attention of the audience on the scene outside then a person by the window might be in semi-silhouette, but the lighting and focus would strongly favour the out-door scene.

In another scene where the background is secondary, lighting and focus would be on the persons inside the room.

Moving Lights During Take

Lights which are to be moved during the take may be attached to the camera, the truck or on lighting booms. A small filler light may be attached to the camera and is normally positioned either immediately over the lens or below it, but sometimes to one side.

If the camera has to move in for a close-up to, say, 3 ft for a facial shot this small lamp acts as a fill-in, and it can give a little sparkle to the eyes. It has no power when it is far away and so does not affect the general lighting set up. But a pup or a 250- or 500-W diffused lamp can be very handy for close-up work and compensates for light loss due to obstruction of studio lighting by the camera. In a track shot it maintains brightness as the camera moves closer.

In an exterior scene where an actor is followed in the sunshine a large light tracking over the top of the camera and mounted on the same crane may be used. This provides a little fill-in from the camera position where the subject is strongly backlit or sidelit. An enormous lamp such as a brute may be necessary to combat the strength of the sun, bearing in mind the aperture setting needed outdoors. Working at a setting of $f11$ ($T11$) or more, a brute at least is required to be any use at all. The brute may be mounted overhead or to one side of the camera. A type of rolling hydraulic stand (Molevator) is available for use with a brute.

On a dull day the brute may become the principal source of light. It may be essential to bring this into operation half-way through the scene, as in the previous shot the sun may have been shining and continuity of lighting must be obtained. You can often be surprisingly economical with lighting in this situation especially if only two or three extra shots are needed.

If the subject is two horsemen following the camera and the camera is covering them only down to waist level, the light need only cover that part.

Strict continuity in the lighting must always be maintained, so that such effects as front light, back light, side light, sun high in the sky, the sun behind a cloud or an orange filter for a sunset, appear consistently in consecutive shots. The required lamp may be mounted on the crane for a moving shot but extension poles or tubular scaffolding

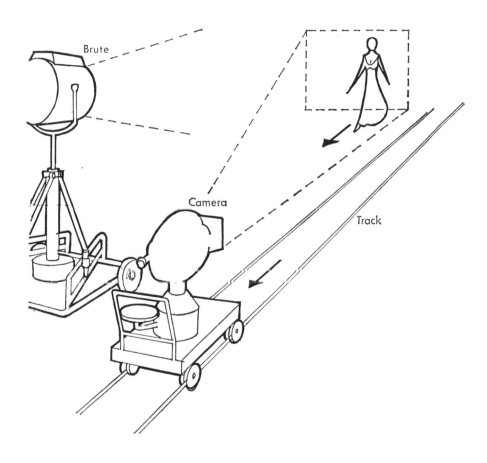

Tracking back before an advancing subject outdoors. The camera tracks are just outside the camera angle; the brute, providing frontal fill light, is mounted on a desert dolly with soft inflatable tyres and no tracks.

may be used to hold the lamp farther from the camera where oblique lighting is needed.

In a studio shot where the camera is tracking at the 4 ft 6 in. level filming two people walking along a pavement, another small dolly carrying the necessary lamp running on a separate track could move along parallel with the camera dolly to provide consistent lighting. Balloon-tyred dollies may be used for the lighting but tracks are laid down where the ground is too uneven.

Moving Light Effect—Static Camera

For a scene where a car passes a house at night and the headlights are seen in the room, a lamp on wheels is run past the window, giving a realistic impression of the car coming from a distance and then sweeping past the house. If the lamp is simply swung round or panned across the window it gives a completely different effect because light comes from the same position all the time and does not give the same impression of movement.

Studio "Night" Lighting

Suppose a character walks out of a room lit with artificial light into darkness and must be seen to look around in, say, the moonlight. The shot may be taken from the outside, though in this particular instance the scene uses a studio set. The outdoor set will already be prepared for night shooting by a suitably painted background or part of a house or wall. This may in some cases be painted as night scenery providing correct tones for a scene illuminated by a street lamp or moonlight, for example. The lighting position for the moon illuminating the road, or the shaft of light leading from the street lamp is obvious. And of course this illumination is darker and more subdued than inside the room. The moon must cast a sharp shadow. This could be provided by a large arc light away up in the roof of the studio which would give a dim but sharp overall light. As the arc light is focused through a lens, it throws a very sharp shadow and by having it at a distance it can cover a large area. You can quite simply diffuse it or dim it down to the strength you require for the moonlight.

The exposure for a character walking about outside must be balanced with the light inside. The general effect must be darker but with enough light to see by. Even if the camera tracks out with the character the lighting must go several degrees darker for the moonlight outside. From experience, the cameraman knows just how much this should be, from the effect of different light levels on the film. It is not possible to be specific about the actual ratio of light levels "indoors" and "outdoors." But a basis of outside illumination at half or one-third the strength of light inside gives some idea of the kind of relationship. There are often many factors affecting these levels, such as the colour of the set outside, the clothes being worn and the basic overall colours that the art director has painted on the set. A whitewashed wall outside on the other side of the street requires the lights to be dimmed considerably to make it look dark but a black wall demands a reasonable amount of light to show anything at all. It is only necessary to think of the wide range of circumstances that could arise to realize that there can be no general ruling for this.

NIGHT SCENES INDOORS—DARKENED ROOM

Night scenes indoors are very rarely represented in total darkness. If a man enters a dark room and closes the door behind him he is, strictly speaking, in the dark. But the human eye (except in people who suffer from night blindness) adjusts itself so that vague shapes soon become visible.

The film sets out to imitate this partial vision in nature. The audience actually has more feeling of a darkened room if some features can be seen than if the screen is totally black.

A totally black screen is meaningless and gives the eye no scale of values which it can comprehend. It only draws attention to the technical failings of cinematograph film—as the screen is not really black but dark grey. Onlookers may become more conscious that they are watching a film rather than taking part in a story.

The story may say that someone is seen in the darkened room, lying asleep on the bed. The lighting is based on that requirement— a dimly lit figure and some shadowy parts of the room. Moonlight, or a street lamp would provide an excuse for light entering the room. The room "darkness" must be balanced with the light coming in through the window, to sustain the illusion.

Contrast control in this case is purely a matter of visual judgment. The effect required might be of a little shaft of moonlight streaking across part of the bed, just showing a recumbent figure. The rest of the room could be in complete blackness except, possibly, for a white ornament or a mirror on the wall which is reflecting the window. This mirror does not require any more light to be added to the scene and the ornament picks up enough light to illuminate itself. The camera-man can make a visual assessment of the suitability of the lighting for these subjects. The mirror may be angled to increase reflection.

A white shawl might be thrown across a chair to give another glimmer on one side to fill a black void and to give a feeling of other things being in the room. A crack of light under the door at the far end of the room might add a sense of dimension to the room. Such small highlights emphasize the darkness in the room.

This arrangement of lighting and props might be built up gradually until the desired atmosphere or composition is achieved.

Night Scenes Indoors—Light Switched On

When someone switches on a practical light in a darkened room the lighting must be arranged so that a main switch is "thrown in" and all auxiliary lighting comes on together, coinciding with the switching on in the scene. It may be necessary to dim out part of the previous darkening effect to avoid conflicting effects or unreal shadows.

For this effect the exposure is set on the camera at a certain level and then the lighting suited to that exposure—the exposure is not adjusted to suit the lighting. Both must be correct for the darkened set and the light scene without any changes. Although the cameraman has some idea of the contrast of the film—which of course has some bearing on this problem—it is more an artistic assessment he is after than a "correct" one.

It is in this kind of lighting situation that experience counts most. The cameraman knows the speed of the film and what he can get at the lowest and highest lighting levels without changing the exposure. He often goes beyond the range of an exposure meter and reaches a point when, although he cannot get a reading, he knows from experience that the effect he wants will appear on the film.

Intentional Reflections

If a person is to be seen reflected in, say, a piano lid, he should receive a good strong key light. Light should be kept off the piano itself as much as possible. There must be a dark area behind him, so that the face reflects clearly in the polished surface. If the person does not appear in the picture himself correct contrast differential between subject and reflection can safely be abandoned and a tremendous light concentrated on him to strengthen the reflection. There may be a strong reflection compared with the brightness of the background behind the subject, but if the camera moves round to one side the background changes, so the lighting must be more strongly focused on the subject to emphasize the reflection farther, to cover views from, or tracking to, other angles.

Exposure depends on the visual aspect of the reflection when compared with the rest of the set and the strength or impact the director wants to give to the reflection. There are several considerations here on the purely practical side.

The cameraman starts off, as it were, "normal" because he already has an exposure in mind for the main part of the set.

To emphasize the reflection by shooting at an angle to the piano more depth of field is needed if the piano is to remain sharp all over. The lighting could be doubled or trebled and corresponding adjustments made to the lens diaphragm.

When focusing on any reflections, the focus distance is from the camera to the surface and then to the subject. It is safest to use a tape-measure for this.

When tracking a camera through a set containing mirrors, take care that the camera, an electrician or stray object is not reflected somewhere. Angle the offending mirror downwards a little whenever possible.

Most sets are built with three walls and a fourth wall floating. The floating wall can be removed for access and is replaced for shots where it is included in the picture. The problem of reflections when tracking past a mirror is considerable because of the constantly changing angle of view and its reflections. So it might be necessary to completely enclose the set with the floating wall to provide realistic reflections in the mirror rather than glimpses of the studio!

BLENDING AND DIFFUSING LIGHT

If a lamp illuminates one person correctly, another person standing half-way between the lamp and the subject is overlit. To the human eye, there is no great difference between the lighting on the two persons, but to the film there is.

This effect is due to the operation of the inverse square law whereby (with a theoretical point-source) the brightness of illumination falling on a subject is inversely proportional to the square of the distance between lamp and subject, so that when, for instance, the distance of the light source from the subject is halved the illumination on the subject is four times as great. By using a more powerful source farther away and thus extending the scale of diminishing illumination an actor can move considerable distances toward or away from the light source without his brightness changing sufficiently to alter exposure. In practice the focusing arc light diminishes the effect of the inverse square distribution because the light is concentrated in a narrower angle than with an open flood, so departing still farther from the theoretical point source characteristics. Fall-off in illumination from any such light source is much less for a given distance of travel than with an open lamp.

Where the exposure is affected by the difference in density due to one actor being much closer to the light source, pieces of diffusing

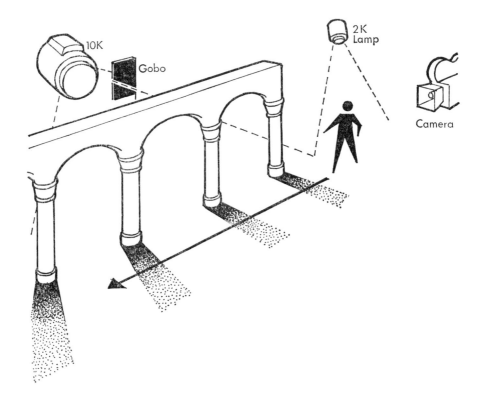

Possible scheme for lighting a subject passing arches on pillars. Movement starts from a position covered by a 2-K lamp placed more to the front than other lamp or lamps. A single 10-K at a distance throws shadows across line of travel (*top*). A gobo ensures a smooth join between the light beams, by controlling the point where one takes over from the other.

material or celluloid may be placed in front of the lamp on double-jointed arms attached to it, which allow small adjustments. Windolite, wire mesh covered with gelatin, can be used in one, two or three thicknesses, overlapping so that the diffusion is graduated across the light beam. Wire gels (gelatin filters reinforced with wire mesh) are more controllable and stand up by themselves. They can be bent as required in any direction. The graduated light beam maintains full strength for the distant subject but reduces light sufficiently on the nearby person to a satisfactory level.

SHOOTING OUTDOORS

Outdoor locations nearly always require additional lighting. Although conditions may be satisfactory for shooting, some improvements are often needed with artificial light.

Broadly speaking, it is handled in the following way. The background is lit by daylight alone. The actors are brought in and take up their various positions. Artificial light is then introduced to improve the lighting on their faces. Sun may possibly be on their backs and extra lighting is needed for their faces, otherwise they will be in silhouette. The lights may often be used to make the director's ideas more effective in pictorial terms, and where, for example, an actor is in the foreground he may be in the shadow of a tree so that he needs extra light to balance with the lighting of other characters in other parts of the scene, or he may need light from a different direction for some other reason.

CHANGES IN THE WEATHER WHILE SHOOTING

With the economic pressures behind modern film production schedules you cannot afford to wait for ideal weather conditions. There may be a large number of expensive actors and technicians working on the picture and no production can afford to have such people idle for long. Actors and technicians have to be paid even if they do not actually do any work. Sometimes the script may permit you to shelve that sequence and start on another. But in the majority of cases work has to continue despite changeable weather. Any sequence must maintain visual continuity unless the script specifically states otherwise.

A sequence which takes a whole week to shoot may in fact represent events in the film taking only five minutes. During this week or during this day as the case may be, there are varying light conditions, starting with the early morning sun and working through the day to the afternoon sun giving strong back-lighting and then low evening light, and the cameraman is expected to use every device to make shooting go on for as long as possible.

To maintain the continuity of either apparent sunshine or apparent dull weather various methods are used.

On some days the sun is constantly going in and coming out. There is a high wind and the clouds are moving rapidly across the sky. The scene can be shot either in the gaps of sunshine or at the times when the clouds are over the sun and everything is in a semi-dull light. This is not as daunting a prospect as one might imagine.

While the camera is set up and the actors are rehearsed the cameraman keeps an eye on the clouds, so that he can prepare everyone for shooting the moment the sun is out or the cloud passes over the sun, as the case may be. He can judge by the speed of the clouds and the size of the gap how long he has for a particular sequence. He eventually becomes a master of judging how long he will have to wait for the next blue patch. He is consulted on the time available for rehearsal, hairdressing or make-up adjustments before the next filming can be done. Sometimes his judgment misfires and the gap in the clouds closes up, but if he is alert, the team can usually get a good day's work done on the patchiest of days.

When the sun comes out after an hour or two of dull weather or vice versa, and filming is already under way, lighting, exposure and often a filter have to be changed to increase or reduce contrast in order to maintain visual continuity.

If a director wants to shoot a sequence that does not suit the mood of the weather he might first talk it over with the director of photography. If, for instance, the sequence to be shot is meant to be spring, he may want it light-hearted, gay and bright. But it is a dull morning. They may wait all day or even two or three days before getting suitable conditions. The director of photography may advise that they make the best of the dull weather. The director might ask what will happen if the sun shines later in the day. The cameraman will do his best to even up the different lighting in this event. There are various tricks for doing this.

He can gobo (or shade) light off a section of the scene either with a large gauze, or double gauze on poles which will cut out the sunshine or cut it down to a soft, subdued light. If that is impossible, the sequence might be put aside and work started on another.

USING REFLECTORS

Sometimes reflectors are used outdoors instead of lights, normally for economic reasons because they do not need a generator. Reflectors can be of more value than brutes because when they are reflecting

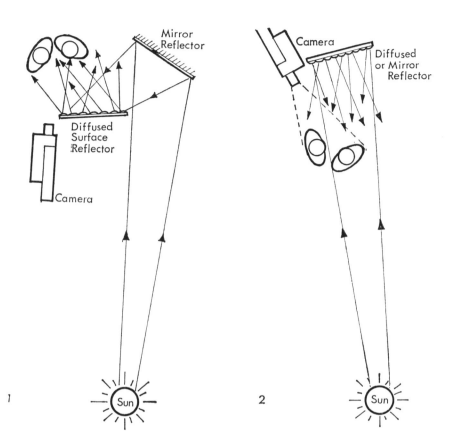

Use of reflectors for subjects outdoors. The sun is far more powerful than any lamps and can be used to fill shadows irrespective of the angle. 1, Working with two reflectors, the first is a mirror surface which directs the sunlight into a diffused surface reflector. 2, The diffused or mirror or reflector is used direct.

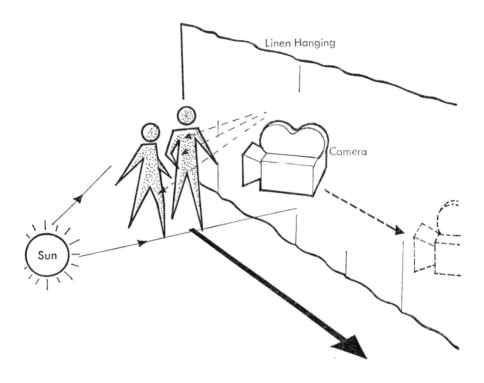

Possible set up for reflecting light outdoors the whole length of a tracking shot. A linen hanging may be erected along the direction of travel throwing reflected sunlight into the shadows side of the the subject throughout the track.

sunshine, they are more powerful. But they do not allow as much control. A skeleton unit working in a remote location may decide to take half a dozen reflectors and do the best they can with those. In a strong wind the reflectors produce wobbling reflections during the shots so they must be well braced. A brute supplies steady illumination in any weather even if placed high up on a tower. But it is wise for the unit to take a few reflectors with them because they have their advantages. The brightest reflector is a large mirror, the next down is of polished metal, or one made from bright metal foil mounted on a flat surface, then a similar device with semi-bright foil and, lastly, just a white sheet or gauze can be placed over the bright silver reflector. A white net can also be used to soften the reflections slightly if they are too hard. Alternatively, a darker coloured or closer net would dim the effect further. The roof of a nearby building might be useful. Two or three reflectors could be used together, as with lamps. In the country a rostrum or the top of a truck would serve the same purpose. In outdoor scenes light from a high position rather than flat illumination is often needed. Reflectors are fine while the sun is there but if it goes behind a cloud the reflector is useless. Brutes can carry on working still and are powerful enough on close-ups to make it appear that the sun is shining.

USING POLARIZING SCREENS

Pola screens are used mostly on exteriors nowadays, to reduce reflections from certain shiny subjects or an unwanted reflection in water or the windscreen of a car, etc. With colour film a pola screen can darken a blue sky. But its application is limited to certain conditions; some parts of the sky contain more polarized light than others according to their position relative to the sun.

Two pola screens can be used together to fade or darken the sky by degrees. They are sometimes made in pairs, contra-rotating in a common mount. If the camera were panned round in a semicircle from a very bright sky at one angle to a dark area at the other the pola screens could be gradually adjusted to compensate and are often used for such a purpose.

Crossing pola screens does not upset the colour balance, but it cuts the exposure tremendously—by at least 4x when fully "open." That has to be allowed for.

Apart from the occasional corrective treatment to skies to maintain even exposure, fades are virtually never done in the camera nowadays, but in the laboratory. Exactly where a fade should come, if at all, is decided by the editor at a later stage. Even so, the cameraman should always have polarizing screens in his gadget box to use when the occasion arises.

7

Camera Techniques

MANY YEARS AGO camera position was determined almost to a formula. The traditional Hollywood school of thought in an introductory sequence, for example, stated that you begin with a long shot, follow with a medium shot, then two over-the-shoulder shots and two single close-ups. That constituted what they called complete coverage of a scene. It may have been fine for a certain situation, but if you saw this going on the whole way through the film it became boring to watch. Up-and-coming young directors soon found methods of breaking away from these well-worn and stale techniques. Another rule stated that you should not jump from one extreme to another. In time this too was successfully disproved. Today there is far greater latitude for the director and he may do what he pleases provided it looks right in the end product. Audiences, also, have exerted their influence and many changes which would have confused them ten years ago are nowadays quite acceptable.

Although camera position is very much the concern of the director, especially when it is related to a certain placing of actors and the atmosphere required, the cameraman can on occasions usefully contribute ideas to improve a scene by giving it a visual "lift"—particularly if the content of the scene is rather dull and static. This naturally depends upon the director; some directors are more receptive to outside suggestions than others where they meet a problem of keeping a difficult scene interesting and alive. The cameraman's experience is always worth calling upon. The best directors realize this and invariably work closely with their directors of photography.

CONVERSATION

For a shot where two people are in conversation, it would not be at all surprising nowadays to see them right in the distance. Their speech might be rather faint though quite distinct but the distant sound of their voices would itself be intriguing. Perhaps at a certain point a third person enters the scene. The two people do not want to be overheard, so in the next shot, which is closer, they lower their voices to a whisper. This style of treatment immediately lends greater excitement and a feeling of expectancy compared with the staid methods of yesteryear.

In present-day practice there may be a hundred different ways of shooting two people in conversation governed by the demands of dialogue, set or situation.

Two-shot Camera Treatment

In a shot of two characters, there are three main factors: a person looking, the relationship between the characters and their points of view.

A person looking may be shot from any convenient angle provided that this relative position remains the same in subsequent shots, e.g. looking left of screen where his opposite number is then seen looking right as they face each other. The camera remains within the near-180° arc to preserve the relative positions for as long as the characters maintain them.

If the characters are presented in long shot, one looking left to right, the other right to left, the camera remains on the same flank of the actors during the whole sequence, that is, it always keeps on one side of a circle. If this rule is not observed, one actor looks as if he has turned away so that both are looking in the same direction.

In those shots which include both the onlooker and the person being looked at, the geography of the set is apparent and the positions of the two people relative to one another and their distance apart is established.

In practice, the first such shot might take the distance between the actors into account and, having established this, a second cut could be made where a change of lens brings an area of special interest closer.

Eye-line

In a situation where a standing person is talking to another who is sitting down, the camera, taking the part of the sitting person must be positioned at his eye level (say 3 ft) and point upwards to the other person. When taking the view of the standing person it must be at his height (say 6 ft) looking down and in approximately the same position as his eyes. The line of sight between two persons, the line where the camera is set for their respective viewpoints, is known as the *eye-line*.

Eye-line shots are all taken in succession from each position so that

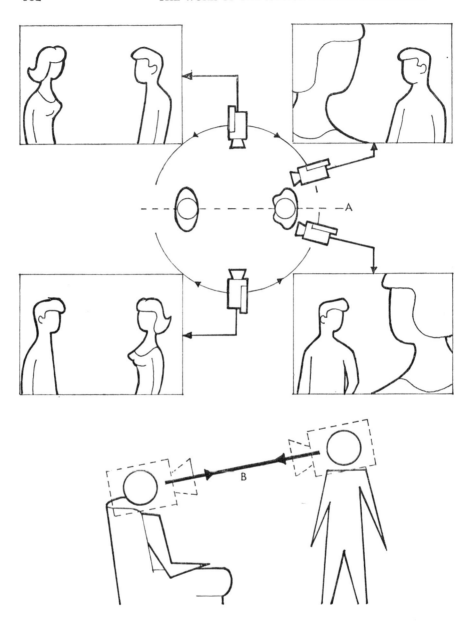

Two-shot camera treatment (*top*). Camera positions must be established on one side or the other of the line A, thereafter keeping within the 180° angle. If the line is crossed, the subjects will unaccountably jump to opposite sides of the screen, confusing the sense of direction. Eye-line (*bottom*) is an imaginary line, B, between two characters placed at different levels, such as where a standing person is talking to someone sitting down. This line corresponds to the line of sight. When taking the view of one character as seen by the other the camera should be placed at the right height, looking along that line.

the camera need be set up only twice. The same goes for over-the-shoulder shots, but with these the eye-line is not used. If it is taken from one actor's position *not showing his shoulder in the picture*, however, it is taken from his eye-line, i.e. the height of his eyes.

In over-the-shoulder shots the other actor does not look straight into the camera but slightly to the right or left Even in those eye-line shots where the shoulder does not show, he looks slightly away from the camera.

Breaking the Eye-line Rule

In a scene where one character menaces another, the old technique of shooting from the smaller person's point of view can be used, placing the camera low and using a wide-angle lens at close range. The aggressor then towers over the camera and if he leans forward his head becomes huge and distorted. Even if the people are of similar stature this technique can still be used effectively. The camera can move from the eye-line of the victim to give a feeling of domination by the other individual. But this difference would be a matter of inches, just 2 or 3 in. either way. The audience would still accept that the two men were looking at one another. But if the camera were to come farther away than this, the visual connection—the whole point of the eye-line rule—would be lost. The choice of angle must be subtle and not make nonsense of the situation presented in the previous few shots. This effect would be reinforced by the lighting.

Camera Movement

There must always be a reason for camera movement with a stationary subject. The director may want to bring the audience closer to the subject imperceptibly with a subtly creeping camera. If it is done very slowly it can be effective. Or, the movement may coincide with the movements of a character. It could be a psychological smash-zoom effect. But the movement must always be justified from some point of view. The dramatic stillness of a scene is easily killed by moving the camera unnecessarily. It is justifiable to let the audience know that the camera is being moved if, say, a man is entering the room and the camera enters with him, shooting from his point of view. But if he was standing outside the door, looking in, his point of view would be a stationary one.

Normally if the actor is standing there looking, his point of view can be shown in a long shot. If he becomes interested in something and peers, the second shot can be closer—showing that he has fastened his attention on some part of the room. It is justifiable to show a closer shot from his point of view. But this should not be by tracking in, because the man is stationary. That would give a quite false impression—the audience would think that he was walking in. This must be avoided.

If the scene is to be carried out from the director's point of view— that is, he is inviting the audience into the scene—then it is a different matter. It is not seen from a particular actor's point of view, and this intention is established beforehand in the shooting.

The audience can be drawn by the director into a room to have a closer look at something. Whether the audience is "watching" or taking the part of the third person is reflected in the camera work. In a scene where there are two men in a room and the camera moves about to the director's requirements, the audience is consciously "watching" the scene. If the director wants to take the audience in closer and show a larger view, he can either make a jump cut or zoom or go in very gradually so that the audience are not aware of the movement. It could be arranged so that when a dramatic point is reached they find themselves very close to it.

There are occasions when the director can go, as it were, between these two approaches, allowing the audience partial involvement. But this is a very subtle method indeed, requiring sensitive direction and camera work.

Close Up

Close-ups of faces involve lighting for portraiture rather than for a set and figures. In fact, in big close-ups the background may even be very far out of focus or excluded altogether. The cameraman concentrates on getting as much out of the eyes and mouth as he can in terms of expression.

In a conversational part of the film, where heads are shown in close up, both heads should be the same size. The same lens must be used, because it has the same characteristics. The lens is changed only if there is some particular reason why the actors should have their attention diverted by something else. There must be a scripted and significant reason for a lens change.

The practised cameraman knows exactly the reproduction ratio that he will get with any lens at any given distance, so that if he were to change lenses and move in for a close up, he would know precisely the position to set his camera.

Except in comedy, an actor rarely looks into the camera. We have established that one person is looking left to right, the other right to left so that even when they look at each other they are still looking slightly left to right or right to left. Rights and lefts in looks or direction of movement invariably refer to camera left or right, not the right or left of the person or object shown. Two people conversing would not normally look alternately into the lens.

If the director wants the audience to participate in the feeling of the complete aloneness of two actors, and he wants to creep the camera in, he has to do it so slowly that there is no feeling of presence at all. The audience must hardly be aware of movement although gradually getting closer to the conversation. Rapid movement would appear quite false. Films have been made in which the camera becomes a person and moves about the room seeing things from the person's viewpoint. This is a rare technique which could very easily be overdone.

ACTION IN CLOSE-UP

When taking an action in close-up it is sometimes necessary to use the movement of, say, a hand, so that it reaches the right position for focusing during the shot. Focus may be switched from one position to another and some permanent mark such as a rod mounted on a sentry stand could be used to guide the actor in his movement. The cameraman might assist by grasping the arm of the actor at the correct point, knowing of course that his own hand will be outside the picture area. This movement could then be repeated accurately each time. Alternatively, he might swing his arm into a predetermined position to meet the actor's arm, while at the same time zooming in with the camera lens so that the guiding arm does not appear in the picture. A high degree of accuracy is needed for this type of shot. If, for example, for effect, the actor's eye is seen through a magnifying glass he is using, an error of half an inch could spoil the effect. After several successful trial runs it is quite possible that he may get it wrong when the camera is rolling! The cameraman has to be prepared to shoot it several times.

In certain close-up situations the camera itself can become a hazard. If for example a tracking shot must take it to within 3 ft of an actor's face there is a danger of throwing a shadow from the camera or its magazine, across the subject. Some prior adjustment to the lights must take care of this.

TILT AND CRANE MOVEMENTS

In a shot where a man is framed full-face in the camera and he suddenly gets up, his position in the picture area can be maintained by suddenly raising the jib of the crane. The height indicator on the crane is marked after rehearsal and the mark gives an indication to the man who is working the lift how far it must be raised. He has to judge the movement—where to begin to slow up—because he cannot come up sharply against a stop that would give a jolt. Naturally the actor must repeat the action at the same speed otherwise the crane operator's rehearsal is valueless. Where the actor jumps to his feet in a very sudden movement a tilt is often preferred because it is rarely possible to raise the camera in the brief time taken by the actor. If a person is seated with the camera more or less level with his face and, as he stands up, the camera goes with him, the movement of the camera is hardly noticeable. This is because the background remains more or less the same; the camera is parallel with the subject and there is little background movement. If, on the other hand, the camera tilts up, the background changes. Perhaps in the first position with the man seated the background is an area about 4 ft up the wall, but the tilt brings in the ceiling. It is a more forceful and more dramatic effect. So you use the tilt for one reason and raise the camera for another.

Pan/Tilt Head

The pan and tilt on a camera is completely manual. It is not heavy to use because the camera mounting is so designed that the camera feels evenly balanced and more or less the same weight whether it is level, tilting up or tilting down. There are different forms of pan tilt head. Some work on a friction principle which partially resists movement. Some are geared so that two handles independently control the panning and the tilting.

The geared type usually has a slow- and a fast-working gear, which is set according to the panning speed needed. The geared head gives a very smooth panning or tilt movement but there is a limit to how fast the movement can be. The friction head allows an operator to do whip pans or sudden tilts, depending on the amount of friction. Slight friction is suitable for rapid movements, but for slower ones the operator finds it easier to get a smooth result if he has to push against a heavier friction.

A camera can be tilted up to the vertical position. The normal camera mounting does not allow this, but small accessory wedges can be inserted to make it possible. A downward tilt to a vertical position can be similarly arranged.

Panning

As with still photography, when panning the camera to follow a moving subject more space is left in the picture area in front of the subject (that side of the screen toward which he is travelling) than behind him, whether for normal or wide-screen composition.

When panning on a subject with a wide-screen camera there is a greater effect of flutter or "strobing" as it is known. If the pan is against a background of regular uprights—say, columns or fences—the strobing or flickering is far more pronounced than with the old format. To avoid the strobing effect the pan has to be very slow or so fast that the background becomes a blur, which always gives a good impression of speed. The intermediate speeds are more or less ruled out against such a background.

Strobing only becomes really distracting with uprights, and it is certainly a nuisance where they are present. If a wide-angle lens is panned at medium speed on a scene of open countryside, the background may look quite reasonable. But if the background is nearby and there are many trees (uprights) the strobing effect is very pronounced. Occasionally this strobing effect may be required on a "whip" pan to give a certain effect but most times it has to be avoided.

If the pan is on a running man and all attention is focused on him— he is steady in the picture frame and quite clear—it does not matter that the background is strobing any more than if it were blurred or out of focus in the normal way.

The strobing effect with cartwheels, which sometimes appear to go forward and sometimes backward, can also be unfortunate, but nothing can be done about it. Strobing cannot really be controlled— just avoided.

The strobe effect can be influenced by the lens, the subject distance, the type of action and the panning speed. Avoiding the unwanted effect when panning is largely a question of judgment—playing with these factors and altering them to suit as far as possible. The effect of blur cannot be reduced by the use of another shutter speed if, in the end, the same rate of panning is seen on the screen. A cine camera exposes 24 frames a second as a standard speed. This is an exposure time of $\frac{1}{50}$ second (or to be precise, $\frac{1}{48}$ second). Although in still photography this would be considered quite inadequate to give a clear picture of a fast-moving subject, for the movie camera subjects appear sharp enough provided that they remain in exactly the same place in the picture throughout the pan. The rate of panning for a particular scene is discussed beforehand by the director of photography, the director and the camera operator and they come to a decision reconcilable with the director's views. He, after all, may *want* the effect of blur in the scene. If the director wants a quick pan which the cameraman knows is risky it would be advisable for him to do one quick one and a slower one for safety. The director can then decide from the rushes which he prefers.

TRACKING OUTDOORS

In a fast-tracking sequence such as a car chase it is perfectly natural to have a certain amount of camera vibration and the shots may in fact be taken from a similar vehicle, using perhaps a stabilizer unit under the camera to even out some of the larger bumps.

For slower-tracking shots, a crane or dolly is used and some pains must be taken to ensure that the camera moves very smoothly. For town sequences where there is a good road surface this may be good enough to dolly along on a pneumatic-tyred vehicle, having let some air out of the tyres to soften the bumps.

In certain outdoor locations with soft surfaces such as the desert a section can be bulldozed, watered down with water-carts and then rolled to make the surface hard and flat. On this surface a large six-wheeled crane can be run satisfactorily at up to 30 mph.

It is more usual to lay tracks down on uneven outdoor surfaces and if they are properly supported all the way along a perfectly flat run is possible.

Many outdoor tracking shots are made with the camera tracking backward in front of the subject. On soft surfaces tyre marks from the tracking vehicle are the obvious result. Where tracks are laid for a dolly these too would show in such a shot. A way to eliminate them is to place the track a little to one side of the subject and shoot it at a slightly oblique angle, just enough to exclude the tracks from the field of view. If a head-on view is essential, a larger crane vehicle can be used with the camera mounted on the end. The end of the boom can be positioned perhaps 15 ft from the track. So with the track offset but the camera running parallel with it the tracks need never appear in the picture. With very long sequences there is obviously a chance of seeing the tracks in the picture, but often such a shot involves a pan round in mid-shot right away from the track altogether.

FOCUSING FOR EFFECT

There are many ways to convey the effect of drama in a scene. The entry of a stranger might be first suggested by a sound effect such as the click of the door. A shot could show the door handle turning. The same dramatic effect can be made with a visual cut from one scene to another. If the sound and visual change is coincidental it forces the attention of the audience onto the subject or dramatic point. This is in just such a manner as the eye would behave.

Throughout a film the cameraman is always switching focus with the camera to imitate the behaviour of the human eye. Only if this is badly done are you aware of it as a mechanical operation. If it is done at the right time with the right intention and combined with preconceived lighting the effect is such that it goes unnoticed as a camera effect but has considerable dramatic potency. Because people in a cinema look at a flat screen and do not view in depth, the eyes are always focused at the same distance—the screen position. Nevertheless the eyes always seek out the sharpest point of the screen image, or rather they are *drawn* to it. This is a fundamental law.

The cameraman must light the people in the foreground of his scene in such a way that they do not appear flatly illuminated. When the focus switches to the background, foreground figures need not appear noticeably "woolly" and out of focus which results from flat frontal lighting. A cross light placed so that the side nearest the camera is in shadow makes the focus change less noticeable than if flat frontal lighting were used. It is normal to avoid large out-of-focus objects in the foreground. But if these large objects are thrown into silhouette they do not really look out of focus. They present a silhouette bulk which, although out of focus, does not draw attention to itself. A large white object in the foreground, frontally lit and out of focus is very noticeable because, in spite of the change of focus to the background, the audience still looks at the very insistent foreground. Errors like this are sometimes not so much the cameraman's fault as that he has been rushed on a low-budget film and has not been able to do all the things he would like to have done.

Deep focus

The purely practical aspects of obtaining deep focus could hardly be more straightforward. It is simply a matter of stepping up the lighting or relighting at a higher power. *Decreasing* the depth of field can be accomplished by closing down the camera shutter so that the aperture on the lens can be opened. The problem with deep focus is really an aesthetic one: many cameramen feel that deep focus has mixed blessings, that it is unartistic and unreal. The audience is inclined to look at almost any part of the screen regardless of its importance simply because it is all sharp. Shallow focus on the other hand separates the actors from the background. The background in turn, becomes less obtrusive, less important and the director can compel the audience to concentrate on the actors' faces, the area of sharp focus. Where the quality of acting is not what it might be, prominent background features might draw the attention of the audience to the exclusion of the actors.

Some backgrounds are a real hazard to effective camera work. On a busy set, that is, a set which has a lot of bits and pieces distributed around it, there are many positions where a person would appear confused with the decor. These busy backgrounds are not nearly so distracting if they are softly rendered. They can be softened by focus, or by lighting. In close-ups of people control of focus is a valuable asset. The background becomes indistinct and the audience's attention is focused on the face without any distractions. This can be a combination of lighting and focus and composition.

Focus may be used to draw attention to the background deliberately. Where two people are sitting in the foreground and at a certain point a door behind them opens and a stranger appears, the cameraman might use deep focus so that the stranger is sharp as well as the people in the foreground. On the other hand he may make a sudden switch of focus to redirect the audience's attention to the door. These two techniques are constantly in use in film making and if they are applied properly the audience is drawn to wherever the director wants. He and the cameraman should discuss the most effective method for each occasion.

Lighting can play quite an important part in this technique. The director might want to see the door open and a figure appear but not reveal who it is. The figure could be thrown into silhouette in a brightly lit doorway. In this situation an out-of-focus figure would be ineffective. As a general rule it is not a good idea to let these two factors contradict one another. If attention is to be drawn to a subject with the lighting, the subject should not be out of focus.

The approach to this scene may be purely a matter of lighting. When the door opens it can be one character or another—at first the audience is not sure which it is. They would not know, for example, whether it was a waiter or the villain if they were of the same build and both wearing dinner jackets. Perhaps the figure then steps forward into the light of the room and they see who it is. In this way the director plays with the emotions of the audience; the effect is discussed between the director and the cameraman or it may already be written into the script. Here the lighting would determine the drama in the scene and the focus would simply agree with it, not adding any particular significance to it.

An image is generally used to simulate a man's inability to see properly when he is ill, drunk or dizzy. This may be done either by throwing the scene out of focus in the camera, which is not very effective by itself, or by diffusing it in some way, which allows some variation. Perhaps the scene may swirl about in a vague distortion to give the feeling that the man's mind is filled with distorted images.

Focus pulling with action subjects

Whenever a moving subject is followed by the camera, unless the movement is across the front of the camera and at some distance, focus adjustment is always necessary during the shot. Characteristic of the type of action sequence needing quite vigorous refocusing technique is a car approaching the camera from a distance, passing at 10 ft and then disappearing quickly over the horizon. The camera movement must needs be a sudden one. The assistant cameraman, who normally works with his hands on the lens, cannot apply his usual methods here. For some difficult crane shots it is better not to have the assistant cameraman with the camera. The camera may be 10 or 15 ft up. In both these situations the answer to focus pulling is to use a Selsen remote control.

The Selsen control is a small electric-powered unit which fits onto the camera lens and by means of a cable duplicates the focus settings on an instrument that the assistant cameraman, standing some distance away, can adjust just as if he had his hand on the lens.

As the car approaches the camera he makes the appropriate focus movement, and as the camera crane moves along he walks beside it holding focus.

ACTORS' MOVEMENT

The present-day attitude to the actor's movement before the cameras is very liberal compared with times past. Nowadays he is allowed as much latitude as possible so that he can play the scene as he wants—the way he feels. The aim is a naturalness that complements the unglossed realism of today's cinema stories. The main reason for imposing control or limitations on his movements is a purely technical one. He is acting for the cameras and although clever camera work may cover his actions in most situations, there are times when because of the camera or lighting his area of activity must be modified or a particular movement curtailed.

Naturally the director has planned the actor's performance in the knowledge of what is normally possible for the camera. But additional problems arise which are hard to see at the planning stage. A typical example is where an actor comes too close to the camera. Nowadays with wide-screen work this is a point to watch, because there is a risk of having, say, two actors face to face in the centre of the screen and a great void at either side. This sort of problem cannot be solved just by shifting the camera or changing a lens. The whole lighting set-up, framing and subsequent camera movement may be based on this position. Hence the actor is moved and the marked points on the floor which act as his guide are altered. An actor might be too close for other reasons; he may pass out of focus at close range or be incompatible with the the the angle of the lens so that his face appears distorted. Moreover, the lighting in that position may be rather poor.

The director acts as a go-between in these matters, seeing both the actor's and the cameraman's point of view. He will either give way to one or compromise to the satisfaction of both parties. It would be absurd if the cameraman had everything arranged to suit himself and the result would be a very dull picture. Everyone has to blend their ideas and manoeuvre into the best position they can find.

Occasionally it is necessary to "cheat" an actor's position in order to get a realistic or otherwise visually pleasing result on the screen. With one actor in the foreground and another in the background, there is a temptation to move them unnaturally close together, in order to get both in focus. This proximity is not, of course, visible from the camera viewpoint. But it is not wise to do this unless you have to. It invariably restricts the actor in some way or other. Cheating is a last resort.

MULTI-CAMERA SET-UPS

Multi-camera set-ups are used mostly for large crowd scenes, certain musical or dance sequences and some fights. Although quite a common technique in television, the serious dramatic cinema film is usually shot with only one camera, except in the situations already mentioned. The crowd or dance scene may be shot from a variety of angles using different lenses so that the editor may cut from one to the other to increase the feeling of activity in the scene.

The greatest shortcoming of multi-camera work as far as cameramen are concerned is that shooting from so many angles at the same time must involve compromises in the lighting. The main advantage is that a large battle scene, for example, employing a thousand extras, which takes hours to rehearse can be put on film in one take.

The scene is usually planned in detail by the director and the director of photography who determine a good angle for the main camera first of all. This is usually a comprehensive shot showing the whole scene, often with another camera alongside with a longer focus lens for more detailed coverage. Other cameras may be placed some distance away at the sides where their angles of view just avoid one another or actually in the field of other cameras, though hidden from them. They would cover additional pieces of action which would not, however, be specially arranged for them.

While the rehearsal is in progress the director of photography walks around and chooses camera positions. It is rehearsed many times, so he can view it from each position before actually setting up the cameras.

When shooting a scene with five cameras the aim is only for the broad effect. Any special piece of foreground action required—a soldier staggering across the screen with an arrow through him—is staged separately.

On the first day of shooting, there may be a thousand extras, on the second only two hundred and if there is a third day there may only be a hundred, enough to provide a background to the more detailed shots. In this way, money is not wasted. It must be decided right at the beginning how few extras can be used for the full effect. To save extras the thousand who are called on the first day might be dressed first as one army and then re-dressed as the opposing one. To stage a clash between the armies only four hundred may be re-dressed. With a variety of camera angles to choose from it is possible to give the effect of ten thousand people. Shooting these scenes always involves giving the impression of more people than are actually present. Costumes are expensive for such large scenes, so the tendency is to work with the minimum of extras.

Scenes in which the set must be burned or blown up call for multi-camera treatment, because they are unrepeatable and, an additional problem, they cannot be rehearsed.

CONTROL OVER A CROWD SCENE

In a crowd scene, the director usually gives an approximate placing for everyone. Sometimes he might just tell everybody to go wild. But after rehearsal certain changes have to be made. Some people must be told what to do because in a crowd there are often one or two people who try to get noticed. They will hurl themselves into the foreground hoping they will catch the director's eye and he will think they are marvellous. In fact, they make a nuisance of themselves, and are usually winkled out and put right at the back.

Even the most relaxed or apparently disarranged crowd is, in fact, a fully organized entity.

THE INDIVIDUAL IN A CROWD

There are several ways of drawing attention to a person in a crowd. He can be brought out with a light, so that he is slightly better lit than the surrounding people. Sometimes a gauze with a hole cut in it can be used to draw attention to one person by keeping others slightly soft. Focus can be centred on him so that he appears sharper in the picture than anyone else. These techniques can be combined for the same effect.

Often the scene represents the point of view of one particular person watching another. In a night-club scene, it may be necessary to pick out a girl from among others dancing in the middle of a circle of tables. In a preliminary long shot the onlooker gets a long view first, then a close shot of the girl.

CATTLE STAMPEDES AND MOVEMENT OVER THE CAMERA

There are several ways of shooting a stampede or a scene where tanks rumble over the camera. A small pit is dug and the camera lowered into it, leaving an opening just sufficiently large for the lens to shoot through, but not large enough for an animal to fall into. There is still a slight danger of the animal's hoof hitting the camera. A thick piece of plate glass can be placed over the aperture, the front of the hole being slightly lower so that the camera can take in an oblique view. The pit may be large enough to take the camera crew also and they are protected by a strong roof constructed from stout boards. But cameramen have been injured and even killed shooting in this way.

To save risking anybody's life a smaller camera such as an Arriflex can be used with a remote control starting device.

EXPLOSIONS

Violent scenes such as explosions or car crashes can also be shot with remote control or angled mirrors. Explosions particularly are a hazard because, although they are not often as powerful as the real thing they can kill anybody who approaches too closely. Unfortunately they rarely look effective unless the camera is quite nearby.

Where accidents are deliberately staged there is often an element of risk and camera crews become accustomed to it. But of course they realize the dangers and take any possible precautions. With a multi-camera set up on an explosion, sandbags and plate-glass camera shields may be used and director's cue lights set up to give the order to roll the cameras.

Every precaution is taken to protect the camera but even so it is frequently the chief, one hopes the only, casualty. Being in the most vulnerable position it can be knocked over, smashed or fall into the sea and be lost.

ANIMAL SEQUENCES

The animals used in films are invariably trained, and people can usually be found who give animals the right kind of training. "Lassie" the famous film dog went on for several generations, his sons or daughters taking over in later films in that series. Other animals might be induced to follow an actor by planting bait on him. But usually the trainer is just behind the camera telling him what to do.

A dog is filmed at dog's eye level unless the human viewpoint is necessary, in which case he is filmed from about 5 ft above. Such a shot shows only the ground immediately around the animal, whereas from his own level the distant view, which may include some useful background features, is visible.

A film in which the dogs only appear would be shot so that the audience is not aware of the camera. The camera tracks along the road with the dog or pans across a field, following him with a long focus lens.

Air to Air Sequences

Most air-to-air scenes are shot with real aircraft. Models are hardly convincing enough for today's large screen cinematography. A plane must be roomy enough for the camera to shoot from the cockpit or side ports. Special brackets are sometimes provided as a rigid camera mounting and, if possible, a section or window is removed so that the camera has an uninterrupted view out. Shooting through the Perspex (Plexiglass) canopy of an aircraft can cause nasty reflections, but if the lens is very close to the Perspex this is greatly reduced except at certain angles to the sun. A pola filter is worth trying to overcome this snag.

When filming in colour at high altitudes, there is generally no problem but in certain conditions a haze filter can be of use.

To counteract the effect of vibrating, especially in helicopters, special mountings are used for the camera. One is known as the Tyler helicopter mount, but with jet aircraft vibration is minimal. When shooting from a helicopter the rotor can be trimmed to reduce vibration while the camera is running. The pilot must be expert and preferably have done plenty of film work before so that he understands exactly what the camera operator is trying to achieve and so flies the plane to suit his requirements.

It is often more convenient to use a hand camera such as an Arriflex for aerial photography because it is smaller, and more easily moved about in a small space. But an assistant is required even with a hand camera: there must be a focus puller. Aerial filming does not necessarily involve shooting at infinity all the time: the wing of the camera aircraft may sometimes be included. A zoom lens is often used to obtain close shots of other planes as it would be extremely dangerous to fly too close together. In the film *The Battle of Britain*, an American B25 plane, with camera mountings in the nose, tail and amidships, was used.

Composition

Although this is an overwhelmingly important aspect of camera work it is probably the one subject which any cameraman is least willing, or even able, to talk about. It has long been said that composition, the arrangement of subjects inside the frame area, is a natural gift — a feeling that things are somehow "right." Formal composition can be learned to some extent from such formulae as the intersection of thirds or the balance of objects in a rectangle. But somehow these only apply in circumstances where particular kinds of subject arrangement are in demand. Cinematography deals with a rather fluid form of arrangement, and the nearest one can come to telling a would-be cameraman what to do is to say that his shots, whether it is the camera or the subject that moves, should flow from one "good composition" to another. The audience is subconsciously aware of composition. But to find composition pleasing is not necessarily the same thing as knowing how to find a pleasing composition. Art primers may help, a weather eye open for the work of others may help more, but the feeling for framing a moving subject satisfactorily within the several shapes of format in use today, only comes with experience behind the camera itself. When wide-screen cinematography was first introduced, it took even the most experienced cameramen time to discover its full potential.

But composition is not simply a question of searching for a beautiful picture. Practical considerations must take their place. The opening to a scene might be a long shot followed by close shot and then various angles round the set, but as pointed out elsewhere this very traditional approach finds few adherents today.

Another opening shot might start in a close-up, on a telephone for instance, and then gradually move away backwards and sideways, perhaps moving almost in a circle. Actors might move around so that the cameraman is, in fact, working in a complete circle, and the lighting must be arranged accordingly.

Composition with a Moving Subject

Satisfactory composition is not necessarily achieved by bringing the camera to a good angle or position on the subject. With a moving subject the possibilities of camera movement are, if anything, more limited than with a stable one. Another way of bringing about the correct framing is to move the subject within the picture. If, for example, an actor walks through a doorway into a room, the point where he is going to stop can be very simply arranged beforehand. He might stop at the corner of a desk, or with a chair on his left—he might even put his hand on it—some natural posture that puts him into a good composition. A good actor who is also a good technician will come to like working this way in the end. These two things, assimilating the mind, and creating the physical action, are very closely allied. The technique in acting, movement and bits of "business" that an actor has to do, help him in this interpretation. Smoking the cigarette and flicking the ash are not adjuncts to the action, they are a normal part of it, and a very visual part that enables the cameraman to put it on film—a physical action—something concrete—something the camera can pick up and make use of.

At the end of a speech the actor might wipe his brow. He doesn't do this in one take and not in another. After several rehearsals the camera-man knows on which line he will do this and at what point he will tap the ash off his cigarette. For the director, these actions become natural

Page 177 *Treasure Island* (1950) (Walt Disney) Robert Newton as Long John Silver and Bobby Driscoll and pirates.
Page 178 *Mogambo* (1953—MGM, John Ford) Clark Gable and Ava Gardner and Page 179 close up of Ava Gardner.
Page 180 *Lawrence of Arabia* (1961—Horizon/Columbia, David Lean) night shot. Peter O'Toole dismounting.
Page 181 *Doctor Zhivago* (1965—MGM, : David Lean) Spain: Cavalry charge across frozen lake. Page 182 Buggy approaching summer residence.
Page 183 Refugees and Ambulance. Page 184 White Russian Cavalry in woods showing mist effect. Page 185 Moscow street (Madrid, Spain) set; night exterior
with artificial snow. Cavalry charge on to rioters. Page 186 Omar Sharif and Julie Christie. Page 187 Rod Steiger and Julie Christie.
Page 188 *Ryan's Daughter* (1969–70—MGM, David Lean) Sarah Miles as Rosie Ryan; West coast of Ireland. Page 189 John Mills following Christopher Jones.
Page 190 Sarah Miles and Christopher Jones. Page 191 Barry Foster and Lee McKern.
Page 192 *You Only Live Twice* (1967—United Artists) James Bond set at Pinewood, probably the largest of its kind ever built.

cutting points, the culmination of a scene, or some intermediate action between one line and another.

The actor is given the first choice of carrying the action out the way that he feels, and, if it is reasonable, that is the way it is filmed. But the cameraman might be able to tell an actor that it would be improved if he hit a position 6 in. to his right or to his left so that he doesn't pause where the background gives trouble. The lighting is arranged so that he moves with good light when he reaches the predetermined spot.

BACKGROUND IN THE COMPOSITION

If an actor chooses the wrong position to stand on the set, a background object may interfere with the composition and have a disturbing or even ludicrous effect. From the camera viewpoint a lampshade in the background might appear to be growing out of the top of his head or an ornament protruding from his left ear. In the terminology of the camera operator he is *wearing* that lamp. In the cinema far more than in still photography one has to be aware of composition in objects as well as lighting. The whole thing has to be controlled; it is fluid, the movement is there all the time. The people and the camera are constantly moving about, and one must try to find a good composition without a clutter of things in the background.

USING FOUR WALLS

Only very infrequently are all four walls of a room used. It is quite tricky because it means that the camera, the director, boom operator, focus puller and all other personnel have to be in the middle of the floor and the camera must be able to move in a complete circle, with these people at the back of it all the time. It is really only done if there is good reason. In a dance sequence, it would be appropriate to revolve the camera, following a couple round the room. It helps in a fast dance sequence where the people are almost giddy, because it accentuates the speed of the dance.

Lighting for such a revolving shot can come from the rails above the set, where there is no interference from cables and stands. It can be arranged to cover a complete circle. But care must be taken that a shadow of the camera is not thrown on the actors' faces, because they might at times be only a few feet away from the camera. A filler light can be positioned beneath the camera, immediately (and exactly) under or over the lens. The cable for this lamp can be wound round the camera tripod several times beforehand so that as the camera revolves it will not be fouled up by the cable.

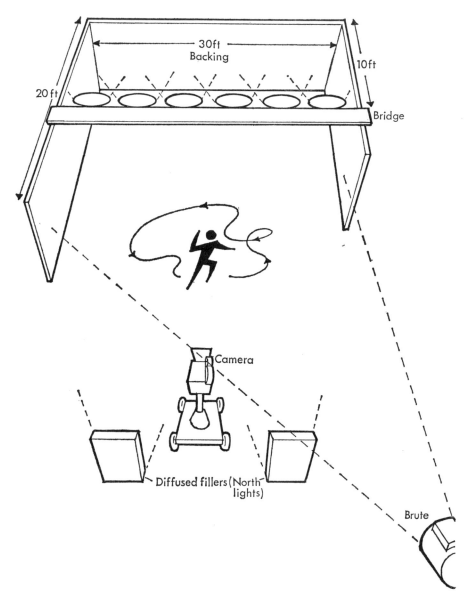

Possible basic arrangement for a dance routine, where a single main lamp keeps shadows simplified (by throwing only one shadow). But, being at some distance, it provides a considerable area of subject movement within which there is little change in the intensity of illumination. The backing is lit by several skypans on a bridge level with the top of the backing and about 10 ft distant from it.

THE INTRODUCTION OF WIDE SCREEN

The introduction of wide-screen cinematography commercially was preceded by a period of vigorous discussion among pundits of the technical world. A number of meetings and lectures were organized in Hollywood where attempts were made to relate the theory of human vision and hearing to the future demands of a cinema audience, and the technical potential of the film medium itself. The movement toward a new, bigger and better cinema came about primarily because of the impact of television in the US and the detrimental effect it was having on box office receipts. It was felt that the only way to compete with the attractions of TV was to exploit to the full the quality and realism which the cinema could impart to the moving image, and the possibilities of the latest advances in high-fidelity sound recording and stereophonic sound. For a time the impact of a variety of new systems, each backed up by effective publicity campaigns, succeeded in winning back the old audience. As time went on wide-screen cinematography became accepted as the assumed medium for all full-length feature films with any pretensions.

Investigations into the uses of the wide screen were paralleled by a growing interest in 3-D and for some time the two systems competed for favour, a number of commercially produced films being released and attracting considerable public interest at the time. But, as everyone knows, wide screen won the day—the system that gave the nearest possible equivalent to the peripheral vision of the human eye.

Peripheral human vision is interpreted in cine terms as the effect of an 18-mm lens giving nearly a half circle of sight with a 100-mm lens in the centre. The half-circle vision was indistinct, a vague sensitivity to objects at other sides of the immediate point of interest. The object you were actually looking at was not only distinct, but your perception of detail in it could only be matched cinematically by a long focus lens.

This information was of a great deal of interest to a professional photographer. In the past, the 50-mm lens was considered the equivalent to human vision, but the theory of the peripheral view plus the enlarged centre now makes wide-screen cinematography a natural advance with great potential.

The new enlarged screen system that would combat television had to be one that could make use of existing cinema structures. There was a limit to the upward growth of the screen due to the balcony level. It was logical then, to grow sideways. The result has been a number of wide-screen systems of various proportions, and the modern cinema is fitted with a masking mechanism that can be adjusted to any of the proportions necessary. These sizes include screen proportions of 1·65:1, 1·75:1, 1·85:1—and from there to the anamorphic or CinemaScope lens at 1·33 : 1 and Cinerama at 3 or 4 : 1. Originally three cameras, and three projectors, necessitating three separate prints, were used for Cinerama. This required the removal of several rows of seats from the stalls to accommodate the projector booths. But now an Ultra Panavision lens is combined with squeeze in the printing to gain the same result with one projector and one film.

WORKING WITH 65/70 MM

In the 70-mm system, shooting is on 65-mm camera negative which is subsequently printed on to 70-mm positive to include space for the sound tracks.

The technique for working with the 65/70 system differs from that of narrower gauges in several respects.

The lenses used in 65/70-mm work are of longer focal length compared with the equivalent lenses for 35-mm film (to cover the same field) and therefore have a shallower depth of field. To increase the depth of field it is necessary to stop the lens down. Hence, more light is required to illuminate the scene being shot than would be the case with 35-mm film.

Another consideration is the movement of actors across the screen. On the wide screen the "flutter" effect with movement is more apparent than on 35-mm and to avoid it the action sometimes has to be curtailed.

The effect of flutter is caused by the destruction of the illusion of continous movement created by "persistence of vision." An actor crossing in front of the camera and at right angles to its shooting direction produces a length of 35-mm negative in which his movement has advanced a fractional distance, say, $\frac{1}{50}$ in. in each frame, roughly equivalent to his crossing the frame in 2 seconds. (In each exposure the shutter is open for $\frac{1}{50}$ second or closed $\frac{1}{50}$ second). He therefore crosses the 35-mm frame (actually 0·86 in. wide) in fifty jumps of $\frac{1}{50}$ in., and is slightly blurred due to the distance he moves during that $\frac{1}{50}$-second exposure. Now, consider the same action photographed on 65-mm negative with twice the width of negative area. To cross 2 in. of negative area in 48 frames (2 seconds). The physical distance advanced in each frame is now $\frac{1}{25}$ in. and his image is twice as blurred although the actual exposure time is the same. While persistence of vision will accept the effect in 35-mm ($\frac{1}{50}$-in. jumps in the image) it will not accept a $\frac{1}{25}$-in. jump (both of course magnified many times on the screen) and so the illusion is partially destroyed—giving rise to the effect known as "flutter."

When this problem occurs with movement across the front of the lens, the director must slow the actor down or give him a more diagonal movement where the flutter is less likely to occur. This can be a little trying for actor and director, but it is essential. Some tests are necessary so that everyone becomes acclimatized to the wide-screen medium.

These factors also apply to Cinerama.

With 65-mm film a longer focus lens is used than on 35-mm for the equivalent area of subject. A long focus lens slows down movement away from or toward the camera lens and tracking appears much slower with a longer focus lens than a wide-angle one. With a wide angle the subject appears to move much more rapidly toward the camera. A director sometimes uses this for dramatic effect—the subject appears to be looming up very suddenly in front of the camera.

The difference in tracking with wide-angle and long-focus lenses is of course a question of viewpoint, not lens. If the track were the same it would take the same time whatever the lens, but at close range the change in size is rapid and the distance covered therefore seems greater.

Lighting technique for wide-screen work is basically the same and looks the same as with 35-mm but as more lights are used to cover the subject there is a greater problem with shadows.

There is no increase in picture height with wide-screen cinematography so the microphone can be roughly in the same place as with normal film. Naturally, with more lights in use there is a greater chance of catching the microphone boom and throwing its shadow onto the set.

8

Filming Studio and Location Effects

A GREATER USE OF real locations rather than mock-ups has tended to shift the emphasis for "effect" scenes also, from studio to field. Both the need for authenticity and a great time/cost saving factor clearly favour this change, even for the largest production. Studio sets are built only where they are really needed.

For the cameraman this tendency means a greater challenge to his abilities. The studio set, as well as being designed from the outset with the effect in mind, offers much greater flexibility in terms of control of effect and resources of lighting power. But this luxury may simply not be worth the trouble or expense. Moreover, it is becoming ever more difficult to produce at reasonable cost a result convincing enough to withstand the scrutiny of modern lenses and film material.

Nowadays, then, we have to consider effects under location conditions as just as important as those obtained in the studio.

TORCHLIGHT

In a torchlight procession or with a group lit by torchlight the torches used are made from padding dipped in oil. These do not give enough light in a night scene except to appear as flames. All surroundings must be lit with an additional source. The faces are generally the main area of interest. With a procession crossing a square photographed from above a light placed at a reasonable height lights all their faces. Extra lights give a basic low level illumination to the surrounding buildings, and a swinging light placed above the crowd lights the front of a building as if it were lit by the torches as they pass close by. The camera position may need to be fairly high to see the depth of the procession and some of the scene behind them.

CANDLELIGHT

In a scene where a person is seen lighting the way with a candle as the only source, some of its light might be expected to fall on the surrounding walls, on the face and the hand holding the candlestick. A small lamp mounted on a dolly or a hand-held lamp moving in front of the person gives the right effect. When the character turns a corner other lamps are brought into play, to give a correct effect of light on each wall and to throw an appropriate shadow of the figure. These lamps are each dimmed or brightened at the right moment as he passes. Further lamps are necessary if the character passes through a door.

A lamp might be attached to the actor's back to give correct illumination on a wall; there are many variations, depending on the circumstances of the scene. If the character is to carry a lantern, a photoflood can be placed inside it. The lead might run up his sleeve and emerge from the back of his coat where it is out of sight. If he walked past a wall there may be a suitable light effect from the lantern, but it is unlikely to be strong enough to photograph in colour, so someone might walk along parallel with him holding a light directed at the wall. If the actor is being followed with lights and he changes the candle from one hand to the other the lamps must follow it, changing the light direction on him, its brightness on the respective walls and the position of his shadow. The supporting lights in a case such as this would of course all be low placed.

FIRELIGHT

In a firelight scene people might be grouped around at various ranges. A low lamp from the position of the fire provides basic lighting; a hole might be dug so that a lamp may be buried near the fire. The light should fall off naturally on the people farthest away. If it falls off too much, another lamp has to "cheat" the effect (i.e. it might be positioned nearer to or even among the people).

Firelight flicker can be obtained in various ways. A torch made of wadding and burning paraffin or oil playing in front of the lamp has this effect on the light beam passing through it. Some thin pieces of silk thread attached to a stick, or a perforated diffuser, can be shimmered in front of the light.

If the scene is at sunset the exposure is based on the sunset and the firelight adjusted for balance.

SUNSET

Artificial sunsets were often used in the past, but today the real thing is necessary.

The point about sunsets is that they do not last very long. Shooting for one scene often has to be spread over two or three sunset evenings. Occasionally the master scene can be shot with a real sunset and then the cross-angle shots where you do not see the sky can be covered later. This could be done with colour gels matched with the sunset on lamps coming from a near-horizontal angle.

The sunset may be good for shooting for as little as a few minutes, so everything must be prepared well in advance for that moment—a moment indeed that may not arrive at all. The sun cannot be photographed when it is too bright or sun spots (or circles of halation) appear over the film. A characteristic of this effect is a secondary image of the sun which appears to the left, right or top of the picture, a fault visible on the film rather than in the viewfinder. Occasionally a rim of light is seen on the film, caused by the sunlight reflecting off the edge of the lens. Such a secondary image is permissible if it is only momentary but it would be a great distraction in a sustained scene.

Paradoxically, in the studio one often deliberately introduces a halo to an artificial sun to give it greater realism. When the sun is a suitable brightness, exposure is based on the sky, but of course any characters in front of it are completely black. Some frontal light on the characters shows detail on their faces. Enough frontal light is needed to show up foreground action. This is not unnatural if done correctly —it is what the human eye would see.

Shooting the sun at dawn or in the evening can be a very trying business. Quite often it means a 3 am call for the crew to get to a location and set up before sunrise. And then if the sunrise is disappointing, to repeat the same call until the required effect is achieved. Sunsets are usually more colourful and more prolonged, and if there was no foreground action required a sunset could be cheated for a sunrise by turning the camera in reverse, or reversing the film in the printing in the laboratory. Sometimes for some technical reason or other the film is "flopped" in the laboratory from left to right or right to left, which is quite acceptable provided there is no lettering or impediment that would give the trick away.

SHOOTING INTO THE SUN

Even the combined effect of a large pack of neutral density filters over the camera lens, and a reduction in exposure does not necessarily cut down the light sufficiently for filming clouds passing across the sun. At its zenith the sun must also be partly obscured otherwise it is practically impossible to film. There is a danger of damage to the camera or film when pointing it at the sun in such conditions. If, on the other hand, you place too many neutral density filters over the lens the result is a small white spot with everything else completely black. The aim should be to strike a balance between sun and sky. There must be some feeling of a blue sky if clouds are to pass across it.

But first it must be decided which lens is to be used. An ordinary lens, such as a normal or wide angle, makes the sun look small and insignificant. A telephoto lens is better, but this is quite tricky to use. When the sun comes into the viewfinder with a tele lens it nearly burns out the cameraman's eye. If he sees a cloud coming and thinks it worth a try, by the time he has chosen a lens, turned the camera in that direction, set the exposure and fitted the appropriate filter the cloud has gone by. No one would say that filming the sun is easy!

On a winter's day when the sun is weak enough to look at with the naked eye it is simple to photograph. If the requirement is for a shot of the sun at its height over the desert, the right effect can be obtained only by trial and error because it is not merely a matter of exposure. On seeing first results, the director might say that it does not give him the feeling that he wants. So various methods must be applied. It may be worth trying, say, to shoot through a pola screen plus 100 per cent neutral density filter at $f16$ and instead of shooting at the middle of the day try at four o'clock in the afternoon or nine o'clock in the morning, depending on the amount of atmosphere and the blueness of the sky at these times. These natural characteristics, too, vary from day to day. Frequently, the chief problem is that the sky comes out white instead of blue. It is always rather tricky to get this correct, several takes are usually shot at different exposure settings. Overexposure produces a large area of glare on the screen and the sun is not visible. It is possible, in the right circumstances, to show the sun surrounded by blue sky.

When using long lenses the rotation of the earth is more apparent and the sun can move out of view during the time it takes to set up the camera.

One method of reducing the brightness ratio of sun and sky is to shoot through a sheet of plain glass with a neutral density screen glued in the centre. This can be lined up in front of the camera so that it fits exactly over the sun. Even so the sun may soon creep round the edge of the screen, so continuous readjustment is necessary.

As a last resort the effect can be done in the studio, on a screen, where you have some measure of control. A spotlight can be positioned behind a screen or blue backing. Or a hole can be cut in a section of blue background and a light placed behind it.

"Day for Night" Photography

If the scene to be shot covers a large area showing distant mountains or countryside, and that scene is a night-time one, then the cameraman must resort to "day for night" technique.

This is a deliberate alteration in camera exposure away from the normal setting required in a daylight scene of given brightness. Such underexposure results in a darkening of the screen image, which in the right circumstances gives the impression that the scene was shot at night. In a scene shot in sunlight, underexposure plus filters causes the sky to darken, and the sun becomes the moon. The highlights from the sunlight in the subject become highlights from the moon.

The most usual methods of changing camera exposure in day for night photography are either to close down the camera shutter or put filters or pola screens in front of the lens, or use a combination of both methods.

A night scene cannot usually be shot in real night conditions, except over a limited area when additional lighting can be brought in. This is an expensive business involving arc lights and powerful generators with a large crew. It also means losing a day beforehand (rest period) and another day at the end of night shooting for rest before going back to day work again. So night work has to be carefully considered and scheduled by the production manager to terminate possibly on a Friday night to allow the weekend to intervene.

In the cinema, a night scene is never completely black. It is the highlights that make us aware of it being night-time, and these highlights are necessary to see any action in the scene at all.

Day for night technique varies according to whether the shot is black and white or colour. With both, the sky represents the biggest problem, because it is so bright in comparison with the scene. With black and white film, a filter (say in the red–orange group) can be used to darken the sky. A cloudless blue sky will be totally effective. But large white clouds would still be bright and here the effect could be more like a storm than a night scene.

In colour this is not so easy. It is possible to use graduated filters, i.e. filters graduated in neutral grey from the top downwards, where the top is the most dense. But the camera cannot be tilted while shooting with a graduated filter. It shows as a filter effect as distinct from the scene itself. A pan shot is possible. These methods of underexposure must be used, or, a higher viewpoint is selected and the camera pointed downward, excluding the sky altogether.

RAIN

When rain sequences are required for a film, it is no good relying on the weather, even in England! The usual method is to use a system of perforated overhead pipes supplied by a high-pressure water unit and with adjustable nozzles to give fine or coarse rain. A wind machine is used to blow the rain sideways. When working in a large area rain might be provided by the local fire brigade whose hoses project the water upwards in a fine spray so that it falls over a wide area.

Before the scene is shot the fire engines first spray the whole area to be sure that everything *looks* wet. In a rain scene there must be rain in depth and not just in front of the lens. On location a rain machine is brought along to provide the effect for the immediate foreground. The fire engines provide the depth behind this.

In the studio, overhead pipes are set up covering the required depth and wind machines are brought in. Fire-hose appliances cannot be used because of the danger to lamps. Spray must not reach the actual lens of the lamp which would immediately crack. Outdoors if rain is at all likely, electricians should always be ready to cover lamps.

When shooting in real rain guard against the camera getting soaked or rain reaching the lens; suitable covers should be handy. With an artificial rain set-up a small fan can be fitted to keep spray off the camera lens. If the wind machine is behind the camera, this helps. In a rain sequence it is much better to have no filter or screen in front of the lens because droplets on this show up much more easily than those on the lens itself.

Unwanted rain does not present much of a hazard unless it is heavy. Fine drizzle on a dank day would probably not show on the screen, and in such circumstances shooting can continue. After a heavy downpour on a "dry" scene, surface wetness on roads, etc., can be removed by throwing down sawdust and sweeping it away again several times.

Falling rain can sometimes interfere with the sound recording. The microphone is covered over. Raindrops sound much worse on the recording than in reality, and where there are noisy places a rubberized horsehair mattress is laid on the ground to absorb the sound of the splashing.

LIGHTING AND SHOOTING RAIN

One problem with rain is to arrange the lights so that you can see it clearly enough. The technique is basically to backlight it for it to show. The difference in the quality of the rain—if it is meant to be a drizzle or a downpour—depends on the angle at which the lighting hits the rain. It is, of course, also related to the tone of the background, a dark one naturally shows up the rain more. A good depth of field is needed for the rain effect, but bold background or foreground effects which are out of focus can still be seen clearly enough—for example, a dripping roof supplied with water from a fire brigade hose, seen in the background.

The rain must appear in depth even if the actors are only 5 ft from the camera.

Lighting Night-time Rain Sequences

A rainy night sequence is backlit also but care is taken to prevent the beams of light from the lamps being picked out by the rain. The lamps should be spread and diffused and positioned where the beams are visible, as with lighting fog. Reflections from wet surfaces can look very effective provided they are lit in such a fashion that the reflections look real. In a street scene the lighting imitates the reflections given by street lights. Methods used are closely related to the economics of the film in question.

Rain in the Studio

Rainpipes are not a permanent fixture in a studio. A large studio has the pipes in their special effects store, to be erected as required. The special advantage of studio rain is that it can be much more easily regulated, and it certainly has to be regulated. To protect the wooden floor of the studio tarpaulins are first laid down and the water runs to a drain and out.

The first rainpipe can be near the camera with a shield so that it falls just in front of the lens. The rainpipes must not cast shadows across the set, and this should be carefully checked.

Nowadays with personnel mostly employed on a freelance basis, the scope for making special gadgets for use in effect shots such as rain is limited by time. You may go out without any thoughts of a rain sequence, and, because of the bad weather, include a rain sequence in the film that was never in the script.

Wind Effects

Several types of machine can be used for wind effects in the studio. Where snow is blown up indoors smaller machines are adequate but outdoors a large petrol aero-engine is essential. Sometimes small aeroplanes are used to supply the wind. They would be quite satisfactory for storm scenes outdoors or large outdoor tanks for model

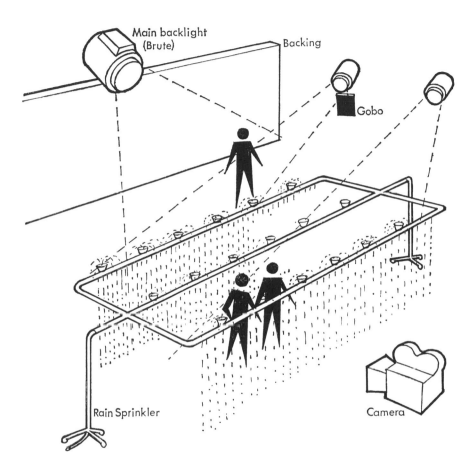

Rain sequence set-up. The sprinkler provides walls of water droplets though the subject may be positioned in a dry area in between the pipes. Backlighting makes the droplets visible but an area is goboed off to enable a subject or feature placed behind the "rain" to be seen through it clearly enough.

shots in a wind-lashed sea, for example. The noise produced by these engines means that soundtracks must always be dubbed on afterwards.

In the studio large wind machines are used only if the whole studio area is needed, i.e. a scene in long shot. But for close-ups smaller electrically driven fans which are comparatively silent are satisfactory, or even very small fans if you only want a slight breeze. Most fully equipped studios offer a range of wind machines in different sizes.

Cloud Movement

Cloud pictures are very rarely shot in the studio. It would be very expensive and they could never be reproduced well enough to look like the real thing. If a shot showing clouds passing across the sun is required by the script, the cameraman has to bear it in mind while filming and be ready to shoot when the right moment arrives. The director and continuity girl should remember that he intends to grasp any opportunity to secure this scene, so they can expect a pause in their work at some point. Often the chance occurs between other shots and the normal filming procedure is not unduly affected. The effect calls for prompt action when likely clouds are approaching. Quite a lot of material should be shot so that the editors can select that most suited to their needs.

When there is very little wind and clouds are moving slowly across the sky, he can reduce the camera speed and adjust the exposure accordingly if the script calls for rapid cloud movement as the prelude to a storm.

Making Light Beams Visible

A shaft of light, sunlight for instance, which is thrown across the set for effect, can be made visible by deliberately putting dust into the air and keeping the lights off areas behind the light beam. This method might be used in a cathedral interior but it is rather difficult. The dust must be there in the first place.

In a studio some powder such as fuller's earth might be dropped from the girders, just enough to catch the light. The beam can then be adjusted to the right breadth and at the time of shooting a further quantity of powder released.

Smoke

Smoke can be used as an effect in itself or simply as a further means to pick out shafts of light. In the second case it can be produced surreptitiously so that no concentration or formation of cloud is seen distinctly. This way it does not look like smoke. The smoke can be made with a small pair of bellows such as those used on bees, with some powder inside which is ignited. The bee-quietening chemical is a good one.

Other methods of making smoke used by a studio include smoke pots which emit smoke of various colours. Chemicals are mixed by special effects people to produce the appropriate hue. The lighting cameraman directs the smoke to the density and consistency he wants for the effect. This may be the normal effect where the smoke rises.

Frozen "smoke" is also used. It lies near the floor in drifts and is produced by another piece of smoke machinery in which oil is forced through a red-hot pipe turning it into vapour. It is then passed over freezing pipes which solidify the vapour, making it heavy and so cause it to hang in the atmosphere. After shooting the sequence fans are used to clear this vapour.

Frozen smoke is often used in dance scenes. There must not be any draughts or currents of air to disturb it—so all ventilators and doors are closed to create the right conditions. This is all rehearsed beforehand, cleared away and done again for the take.

Fog

Fog is often seen over water in film sequences, and for this, the "silent stage" (studio) provides the right facilities. The whole studio can be flooded with water to a depth of about 4 ft. It can be used for shipwreck scenes and so on. There are platforms for the cameras or they can be run on wheeled dollies through the water leaving the camera platform just clear of the water surface. Special effects men produce the fog from smoke machines mounted on movable platforms, which are dotted around the studio. They fill the studio with vapour, taking perhaps 10 minutes or a quarter of an hour to achieve the right density over the entire stage which might be 200–300 ft long and 50 ft high. The vapour then has to level itself out to get the desired consistency. It may be low fog just floating over the top of the water, so one must wait until it settles into position, making sure that there is no movement of air in the studio.

Lighting a Fog Scene

Lighting fog is quite tricky. A light shone into it is reflected straight back. The technique is to light *through* the fog, done mostly by backlighting it or side-swiping the fog with the light. A brute used from a long way off, somewhere at the top of the studio, gives the right effect. This allows the light to spread, and unless it spreads, a distinct beam of light is visible. The spotlight may need to be diffused to spread it enough. This type of light might represent early dawn or moonlight. Working with fog requires almost limitless patience on the part of everyone concerned and they should all wear smog masks to protect their lungs.

SNOW SCENES

A scene where snow is actually falling is not often filmed outdoors for the same reason as with rain: it cannot be relied upon. Shooting a snow scene means thinking in terms of several hours', if not several days', work. The ground has to be covered with artificial snow and falling snow provided from a suitable machine. Sometimes, shooting can be undertaken when there is actually snow on the ground. Then, in a large feature production where there is no shortage of money and staff, a large area which is only partially snow covered may be used. Patches where there is no snow can be filled with marble dust or plaster dust. Other materials may also be used, depending on the nature of the ground. Rock salt, for example, suits some situations. White plastic sheeting can be spread over bushes which are only seen in the far distance. Salt is often more satisfactory than other materials for putting on the hats or shoulders of people in the film and is far more convincing, giving a more realistic glint than marble or plaster dust.

At times the snow on the ground is not thick enough and must be built up in the foreground. Snowfall over a wide area can be produced by the use of plastic chips or chopped feathers blown in from a high rostrum some distance away. A powerful aero-type petrol engine is mounted on the rostrum so that the snow is driven up into the sky and falls in front of the camera.

STUDIO SNOW SCENES

Indoors the set can be covered in various ways to simulate snow. Bare trees can be partially sprayed with white paint, the tops of walls can be layered with cotton wool to give the thickness. In the foreground, where actors have to walk, several inches of salt must be put down so that as they walk, their feet sink in quite naturally.

The snowfall may be done with different materials depending upon the mood of the scene. If it is to be a romantic scene, where the snow falls softly, chopped goose feathers can be used, as these will float gently down in front of the camera. For a vicious snowstorm with a biting wind something stronger is called for, such as cut-up paper, rice flakes or perhaps a mixture of several such materials. The people have salt on their hats and shoulders and against their chests if they are walking into the snow. Snow is driven against them with wind machines.

Another type of machine blows soap flakes into the air under strong pressure. These come down in a way that looks quite natural, and if they settle on people's hats and coats have the appearance of rather wet snow.

These variations have to be considered for the particular scene.

LIGHTING AND SHOOTING SNOW

A snow scene on location provides a strong upward reflection and a reading off the subject gives an exposure to secure a satisfactory picture. There is no problem of contrast between the snow and the subject either in colour or black and white. If the sun is being used as a backlight, some additional light on the faces in the foreground will probably be needed. Reflectors or lights will do. Otherwise, there is no particular technique for lighting snow.

Falling snow, like rain and fog, shows up the light beams from arcs, so diffusion is called for here too. For a snowscene shot in the studio underneath-lighting is usually added to ape the natural effect. Several "pans," large flat reflective lights with 1000 bulbs, would be suitable for these.

In an "indoor" set where snow is on the ground outside lights thrown onto the ceiling and walls near the window are appropriate if the window is large. In front of those underneath the window and just out of sight a scrim of butter muslin can be fitted to diffuse the light, so that it is generally reflective rather than a beam. The lamp most useful for this is a skypan, a light which is generally used for backings where a wide spread of illumination is needed.

COLD WEATHER PROBLEMS

In cold weather, heaters, run from batteries, can be used inside the camera to keep the mechanism warm. The camera should be kept in some warm place until the last moment. The heaters help to retain that warmth. Lenses sometimes mist up when taking the camera from cold conditions to warm and condensation can form between the lens glasses, which takes some time to clear even when the lens is warmed. The lights do not give rise to any problems in cold conditions.

THE SPECIAL EFFECTS DEPARTMENT

Except for optical effects which are done by the laboratory, the lighting cameraman usually likes to have overall control of the photography himself. The special effects department generally uses its own

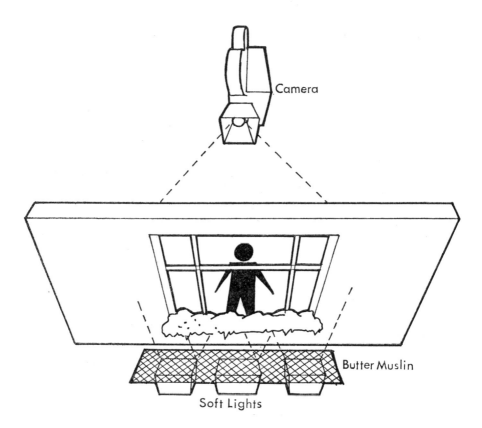

"Snow scene" outside a window throws its own kind of lighting into the room—the only occasion when strong light comes upwards, instead of from the usual direction. Soft lighting is positioned outside the window to simulate this effect.

camera but even so, the director of photography takes charge where any scene involves actors.

Special effects are discussed between the special effects man, the director of photography and the director of the film, during which discussions the work of the effects man is open to comment and criticism from the other two. Several attempts may be made to achieve a result to satisfy all three parties. For the most part and certainly with all the more usual *natural* effects, the director of photography does his own lighting and organizes the effects himself. Such effects as waves (in a flooded studio water sequence) rain and fog are all under his supervision and lighting.

Effects are passed on to a regular second unit only in a crowded programme. Many directors like their effects to be done only by the first unit. Some effects may warrant a second unit and perhaps several cameras shooting at the same time—an arrangement best sorted out with the production manager before filming begins. An experienced cameraman might be engaged for this sequence, and sometimes there is a second unit director.

EFFECTS LIBRARY MATERIAL

Existing special effects from a studio library are snippets from other films and are never specially filmed for library storage. The libraries are often consulted and although quite a large sum of money has to be paid for a few feet of film it is very worth while if it happens to be right. But rarely do they completely suit the film for which they are wanted. There is nearly always something that doesn't quite fit.

FIXED MATTE

The fixed matte is an added section of picture replacing part of a real scene which does not in its entirety provide the view needed for the film. The replacement material may be, and often in fact is, a specially mocked-up, painted or photographed piece of background. An example from the film *Lord Jim* demonstrates a typical application of this technique. A view was required looking across Hong Kong harbour toward the hills on the other side. The film was supposed to depict Hong Kong in 1900 when the far hills were dotted about with cottages and other small buildings. Today, this distant prospect consists of an assortment of skyscrapers.

The camera was set up opposite, on a sea jetty 14 ft high, to give a clear view over the masts of junks, dhows, etc., in the foreground. The top third of the picture was matted out with a black board positioned close to the camera (about 2 ft) and so giving a soft edge. The matte was simply a black piece of three-ply firmly mounted so that it did not shudder in the wind. The camera itself was locked down rock steady. The matte covered the far side of the harbour, so that later on in the process department back in London they could print in a specially painted glass backdrop showing distant hills and scenery as it was in the year 1900.

TRAVELLING MATTE

For a travelling matte shot, the foreground action is first shot against a blue backing specially lit so that later, in the laboratory, a background can be double printed over the foreground action carefully avoiding use of blue colour on any foreground.

Lighting for a travelling matte shot has to be carefully considered, so that the foreground appears to be lit from the same direction as the background. This usually means a correspondence in the position of the sun in both cases. It can be quite tricky to ensure that the shadows in both foreground and background fall in the same way. This must be done together with a balance of exposure of the foreground to the blue backing. The latest method uses a transparent blue plastic backing which is illuminated from behind by hundreds of photoflood bulbs. This is a great improvement on a blue-painted backing which has to be lit from the front.

THE SCHUFFTAN PROCESS

The basis of this old process which is now largely of academic interest, was a mirror set at 45° to the camera lens. Parts of the mirror were scraped away so that in those areas the camera could see straight through clear glass to the studio set which might be 12 ft high. At one side of the camera, reflected in the remaining silvered parts, was the piece you wished to add—it might be a ceiling. The disadvantage with this system was that you could not move the camera. The scene was covered with just one long shot and after that you had to move in to close shots working against the 12-ft background. One particular interior (in the film *Victoria the Great*), the ballroom of Buckingham Palace, was transformed to a night scene by filming a daylight interior transparency backed with tracing paper. It was lit from behind and with the tops of the candles scraped out to make them brighter and a few controlled patches of light added here and there with spotlights, in those days it appeared entirely convincing.

This method has been little used since the war, but some old systems are worth remembering in case they may one day provide at least part of the answer for a new problem in a new situation.

9

Working With Artificial Backgrounds

THE EMPHASIS TODAY is on realism. Production companies tirelessly seek to provide exotic settings for their films, and will move their production teams to almost any part of the world in order to secure an authentic background.

Even so, several forms of artificial background are in current use. It is sometimes more convenient to handle certain parts of a film in the studio, so the real location may also have to be duplicated, or reproduced in part for much of the studio work.

Some studio sequences may not require much background detail, perhaps only a suggestion of the location, but for another scene a large and detailed backdrop may be essential. The method to be used is decided in accordance with these visual requirements, bearing in mind the cost and time available.

As each method demands different lighting technique, the cameraman will be working within strict limitations. But even within this rather tight framework he can bring his own ideas to bear, and an experienced person can enjoy comparative freedom and flexibility.

PAINTED AND PHOTOGRAPHIC BACKINGS

Painted backgrounds were at one time very popular for all kinds of scene, but with the improvement of lenses and photographic materials and consequently a superior image quality, the camera today is not so easily deceived. Whereas in the old days landscape, buildings and other features would be cheerfully included in the painted scene, it is now no longer suitable for such detail. It can, however, provide a handy background fill-in, preferably thrown out of focus, and is still used in this way, for example, where it is vaguely seen through a window. Lighting for a painted background has to be balanced with that on the set in much the same way as for the modern photographic backing.

A photographic backing is a very large blow-up of a picture taken with a still camera. The original negative may be from a camera of 5 × 4-in. format to ensure really good quality when enlarged to 15–40 ft or more. The print, on photographic paper, is mounted on a flat background of plywood or Essex board. It is vital that the surface be perfectly even.

This type of backing is used only where there is no movement involved, for instance for the top section of the Eiffel Tower where the road cannot be seen.

LIGHTING BACKINGS

The backing must be flatly and evenly illuminated. It can be done with lamps at the top, bottom and sides. Open lights (not spot-lights) are normally used because of their diffused illumination. The paper has a matt surface, so there are no reflections and the obliquely angled lights avoid any sheen. A large backing may require fifty to sixty photoflood lamps arranged in banks, but larger "skypans," lamps of 5–10 kW, may be used. These give a wide area of light and when used together create the necessary flat lighting. For a backing of 20 ft width 300, 400 or 500 foot-candles of light may be needed, yet the lamps must be far enough away to be out of the field of vision. The intensity of illumination is most important, but to take into account the total characteristics of the backing as well a *reflective* (reflected light) meter reading would be used, not a foot-candle reading. The term "foot-lamberts" means the amount of light which actually reflects back from the screen.

So the tone value of the backing is taken into account. A basic lighting intensity is evolved and all subsequent lighting on the set should then be related to it. The set cannot, of course, be lit with an exposure meter. The meter gives the strength of the key light and keeps the level fairly even, but the balancing of lights is largely a matter of judgment. The meter is just a guide.

CONTROLLED BACKING LIGHTS

Often, one photographic backing must serve for both daytime and night scenes. The picture on the backing is a daytime shot. During the scene dusk may begin to fall, so the illumination is reduced. Later on, as night approaches, the light on the sky area is shaded and finally thrown into darkness. For the night scene, the windows in the backing may be cut out and illuminated from behind, transferring it into a

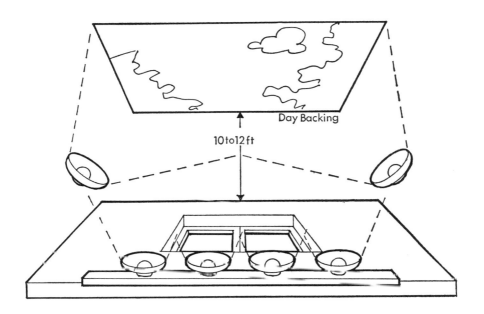

Day Backing

10to12ft

Camera

Window backing (daytime). The window is backed with a painted or photographic background placed 10–12 ft behind the set. It may be lit by the skypans on the floor and three or four placed on a rail above the window.

night backing. There will be practically no light from the front, and the light coming through the cut-outs should be balanced by eye and set to the correct intensity.

In certain circumstances, the background may not be given an overall light, but only lit in patches. For example, a street scene at night supposedly lit by two street lamps would be lit locally, in the areas surrounding the two lamps. One or two "windows" may be cut in the backing and lights positioned behind these. If the scene were to be shot in colour, suitable coloured lights (e.g. amber or pink) would add interest.

Details on the backing are not confined to those of the photographic image. For some effects, cut-outs of the distant skyline or miniature sets may be placed immediately in front of the backing. A large gauze screen hung in front of the backing and/or the cut-outs can help to give an illusion of distance by softening the outline and reducing contrast. The slight loss of definition with this technique accentuates the effect.

Model neon signs might also be placed in front of a night backing and further details built in front of these—a whole miniature set placed before the backing and constructed to give the feeling of depth. A more radical step to take with the backing is to cut out the sky portion and place beyond the buildings a canvas backing lit for the night sky.

A NIGHT WINDOW BACKING

A view of the city at night seen through a window could be built up realistically using as a basis a photographic enlargement outside the window with small holes in it covered over with transparent paper and illuminated from behind. The scene would be mainly dark but with a small amount of detail in the sky and a mass of tiny "lights." Buildings are nearly always silhouetted against the sky. A large sign on the other side of the street might be made to go on and off so a flickering light coinciding with the light would be arranged in the room. One sign itself might be made from "pea" lamps which are about the size of a small pea, made to flash on and off. All this demands quite intricate lighting technique.

PRINCIPLES AND ADVANTAGES OF BACK PROJECTION

With back projection the scene is thrown onto a screen at the rear of the set. The screen stands between the camera and projector which are facing one another on the same optical axis. A slide or "plate," which may be a moving cine sequence, is specially prepared for the

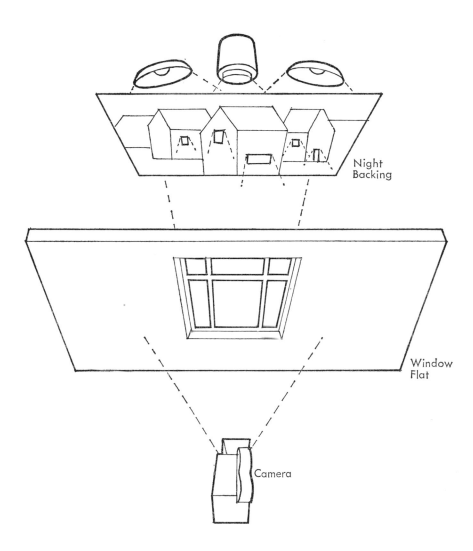

Studio set with night backing seen through a window. Lights may be positioned behind the backing to illuminate translucent features cut out of the background, such as windows, sky, etc. Small lamps (pea bulbs) may be fitted to the backing to represent illuminated signs, street lamps, etc.

scene to be shot. The term "plate" is used when referring to either still or moving projected backgrounds.

The economic advantage of the system is obvious. Only a camera team need be sent to obtain the plate, which may be at a distant or inaccessible location. The setting might be ideal for the film but there may be insufficient foreground space for the action, and all the technical paraphernalia that goes with shooting it. The reasons for using back projection may be concerned with other location problems. One can imagine permission granted for the filming of plates in a particular monastery where the presence of the whole production team would be out of the question. In this way backgrounds can be used which would not normally be available.

A major advantage of the back projection system is that the action can be concentrated in one spot, and full control maintained over it with the convenience of working in a studio. A familiar example of this is where conversation passes between two people sitting in a car which is supposed to be passing through heavy traffic. If this were to be shot in a real setting the shooting and sound recording difficulties would be immense and would probably necessitate post-synchronizing the voices. Back projection provides a simple answer. The car is in the studio and the street scene seen through the back window is a previously filmed sequence thrown on the screen behind. The speech is recorded in the silence of the studio and any car sounds or traffic effects added afterwards.

Back projection may be used in a tremendous range of situations and some films rely on it for a very substantial part of their exterior work. Its use is not confined to small budget films, even first features contain some back projection sequences though normally only in secondary scenes, the main ones using the real location, or part of it, plus a travelling matte (see page 212). Back projection is particularly suitable where small areas of the picture need a projected image (i.e. views through windows etc.). For larger backgrounds front projection, which gives more light, is chosen if the budget of the film allows for it.

PROJECTOR AND SCREEN FOR BACK PROJECTION

The projector is specially designed for back projection work. It has a powerful (225-amp) carbon arc light source with a colour temperature similar to daylight. The power of the light source can be regulated by varying the amperage, or by the use of neutral-density filters. Only a very bright light allows small apertures to be used on the camera to give the considerable depth of field often required. The scene itself might be a bright one such as the view across a beach in brilliant sunshine. The picture when thrown on the screen may be 20 ft wide. People

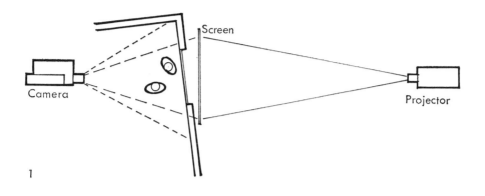

1

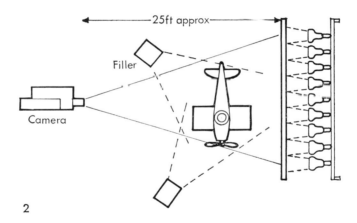

2

Back projection and blue screen photography set-ups. 1, Back projection "plate" is thrown (laterally reversed) onto a screen usually occupying a small part of the scene. The camera faces the opposite side of the screen on the axis of the projector lens. They must share this axis regardless of the angle of the set. There must be enough space behind the set to allow a generous projector throw; too short a throw causes a hot spot to appear in the central screen area. 2, Blue screen photography for travelling matte. The translucent blue screen covers the entire background and is illuminated from behind from a grid of closely spaced lamps. The subject is positioned far enough in front of the screen to prevent light from key, filter or effect lights striking the surface of the screen.

in the foreground in front of the screen must appear sharp, and an aperture of $f5\cdot6$ could be necessary to keep them and the projected image within the depth of field. It would be practically impossible for a single projector to give the light output needed with colour film which has a lower emulsion speed.

Triple-headed projectors have three separate carbon arcs to give a light of great brilliance. These arcs are arranged with one in the centre and one on either side. The light is directed through prisms onto the same film and through the same lens. The film in the projector becomes extremely hot and only the cold air jets passing over it keep the temperature within tolerable limits. A safety gate keeps the light off the film until the projector reaches the full 24 fps running speed. This gate then automatically lifts off. If this intensity of light were to pass through the film when the projector was stationary it would be burnt in a fraction of a second.

During rehearsals only one of the arcs is used, and even this need not be at full power. A fairly weak picture is adequate for a rough line-up.

A range of interchangeable lenses is provided for the projector so that an image of any size can be thrown on the screen. The projector can be moved back and forward, tilted and raised on a rostrum.

The screen may be angled in various ways to suit the scene and the projector position changed accordingly.

The projection screen is flat and without supporting cross struts. It is made from translucent plastic with a matt surface which allows as much light through as possible but has a sufficiently frosted surface to retain an image.

The projector throws a reversed image, i.e. left to right, which when viewed through the other side appears the correct way round. This direction is important because of pictorial details in the plate. Lettering especially must be seen the right way round and traffic must appear on the correct side of the road. If there were no such features to give it away the film could be turned round the other way in the projector. Where a left turn was needed in a country lane that actually turned to the right, the film could be flopped provided there were no tell-tale signs or traffic in the picture. The full aperture frame, as in the days of silent films, is used to give increased picture area and thus increased definition.

The back projection is synchronized with the camera. The shutter on the projector is linked electrically with that on the camera so that they are both open or closed at the same time. The motors work in phase and they start and stop together.

Studio Set-up for Back Projection

The set is constructed with the set furnishings placed in front of the screen. The entire background can be back projection and the foreground in medium close-up, which is satisfactory for any shot down to knee length. For full-length shooting some set piece in the foreground is needed so that the figures appear to be standing on real ground. This piece of set is made to blend into the screen. A sandy beach, for instance, would be laid on a rostrum in the foreground built up to the height of the beach that can be seen projected at the bottom of the screen. The sand in the foreground would be lit to blend effectively into the sand on the screen. Some additional features may be placed at the right and left of the screen, such as a beach hut and some other fixture to restrict view at the sides. Without this arrangement an enormous screen would be needed. To fill such a screen the plate would have to be enlarged to great size, creating a grainy effect which is unacceptable, and destroying the relationship in scale between foreground and background.

The back projection scene is preplanned and the set constructed accordingly. The foreground piece may be a mock-up taxi or car which is probably mounted on rockers so that the vibration of the car can be simulated during the scene. For an open car wind may be provided by a wind machine to blow hair.

The projector is switched on and the camera lined up. After the scene has been lit to unite background and foreground, stand-in actors are brought on for rehearsals and they are then lit. Next, actors are brought in and rehearsed and any adjustments of lighting made, also any test rocking of the car and polishing up of the action is carried out. During these rehearsals a second rehearsal plate is used so that the shooting plate, which is a specially made print free from blemishes is only used when actual shooting is in progress.

Shooting the Plate

Background projection plates are planned in detail before being shot. If additional plates are required during the production a second unit cameraman is sent out. Sometimes plates are shot in bad light and do not meet lighting requirements exactly, but the lighting cameraman is expected to do the best he can: the time factor is all-important. As plates are required only as a background, their subject matter should not be obtrusive. The illusion depends upon them looking subordinate, as in fact real backgrounds are supposed to be. This applies whether they are for front or back projection.

Certain rules apply to shooting plates. No part of the subject must come very close to the camera. For car mock-up shots the view down a street from the back of a car may be required. Other cars following the camera must not come too close or they will appear larger than the car from which they are supposed to be seen.

Angles to be shot are stipulated by the director before the plate is made. If for instance the people in the car are to be taken from several angles the background too must change to the appropriately angled view. With a similar background for all shots the effect would not be convincing. Normally you would shoot one plate of the view straight back down the road, another looking three-quarters back/left and a third plate looking three-quarters back/right. In the studio, when you shoot favouring one person or another, the plate is changed in the projector, to one with a suitable background.

Variety in background features emphasizes the sense of direction. If there are trees down one side of the street and buildings down the other, a change of viewpoint is more noticeable.

The angle shots are critical. If the angle is incorrect the car appears in the end result to be skidding round a corner. Upward and downward angles must also be carefully planned.

A forward-facing plate may sometimes be needed. This would be the driver's view of the road in front, for example, approaching a cross roads where he might nearly have an accident—a car flashing past and just missing him. The studio shot would be made from behind the driver's head.

The height of the camera is very important. The plate must be shot from the level of view adopted by the camera in the studio—in this case the height of the person sitting in the car. This could be tape-measured, or the camera lined up with someone sitting in the car, at a height of, say, 4 ft 6 in. from the ground. The measurement goes down in the instructions on the camera sheet to ensure that the studio camera is not taken up to 6 ft, where it would look down on the subject and make the background look completely wrong. If the plate is shot at 5 ft therefore the projector must be at 5 ft and the studio camera also at this height.

Background projection is often used for aerial sequences. They are shot in the air and a mock-up built in the studio. The actors can appear piloting their aircraft over such features as mountain ranges and enemy airfields. These backgrounds could be provided economically and without sound-recording problems such as you would have in a real air sequence.

Backgrounds for certain front projection aerial sequences in the *Battle of Britain* were shot on 65 mm to ensure that they would show no noticeable grain although the film itself was made on 35 mm.

Library Stock for Plates

A distant location which will appear only very briefly in the film is sometimes selected from library material. It would be an extract from some other film. Many of these special scenes are stored for future use and made available for a fee. The editor might go through a great quantity of library material from other studios in order to find a suitable shot. But he very rarely finds the ideal one. There is nearly always something missing, or something there that he does not want. Generally speaking it is preferable to use frontal or cross lighting for a back projection sequence—it always looks better and helps to disguise the process.

Balancing Background and Subject Lighting

The back projection screen is always used as close as possible to the actors. In a car sequence where the projected scene is seen through the back window the screen may be as little as 18 in. from the back of the mock-up.

Sometimes the background visible through a room window must appear fairly sharp to show certain exterior details related to the story.

Where screen and actors are close together it is far easier to contain both within the available depth of field. However, the lighting becomes difficult because shadows from the actors must not fall on the screen, nor in fact must any light reach the screen from the lamps placed in front of it.

In a setting such as a street scene railings might have to be placed 2 or 3 ft from the screen in order that they, as well as the actors, be properly lit without any frontal lighting reaching the screen. This interplay of lights, screen, distance and depth of field is a large part of the technique of back projection.

The chosen key of lighting for the set is governed by the intensity of the arc behind the back projection screen. This is determined first, then the lighting on the set is balanced with it. There is much more latitude with the lighting inside the set than on the back projection screen.

Lining Up the Camera

In a back projection set-up the camera must be facing the projector square-on all the time. If it is angled away from the direct line of sight the illumination on the screen falls off drastically. When shooting obliquely to the window the screen must be angled accordingly (see diagram). Because of this disadvantage it is often better to use a photographic backing, reserving back projection for scenes with background movement.

The correct optical axis of the projector is indicated by a chalk line drawn on the studio floor from the projector to the front of the set. The camera can then be placed on this knowing that it will always be properly in line. To mark out the straight line a chalked cord can be held across the studio and flipped onto the floor, where it leaves a faint image which can then be painted in.

The studio rostrum is on wheels and where different camera angles are required on a car mock-up the car is turned so that the camera, screen and projector need not be shifted from the white line.

SUBJECT AND BACKGROUND SIZES

When lining up the camera it is essential to maintain the correct size relationship with the background whatever lens is used and at whatever shooting distance.

Suppose a figure in the foreground is framed to knee length and the background is placed at the correct distance. In the next shot the same background is used but the figure is framed to waist level either by changing the lens or moving the camera forward. For this shot more or less the whole screen must still be visible because, despite the change from a knee shot to a waist shot, the background in a real location would not be very different. If, instead of changing the lens, the camera is moved in by about 4 ft, the effect is to mask down the back projected image, giving a closer view of only part of it. This is quite wrong. The background should look the same as for the previous shot. This is done by making the screen image smaller, usually by putting a different lens on the projector or moving it forward. If the screen image is, say, 20 ft wide for the knee-length figure, it may possibly need to be only 10 ft wide when jumping to the waist shot. Therefore a longer focus lens is needed on the projector to bring the picture down to this size.

When shooting a car interior and looking through the back window at the screen, the back window may be only 2 ft or 2 ft 6 in. wide. The screen image would be brought down to about 3 ft for a 2 ft 6 in. window. A taxi window may be only 18 in. wide; the screen image would be reduced to, say, 1 ft 9 in. so that the area of the window is just barely covered.

In every case the screen image is kept down to a size just large enough to cover the area in which it is to be included. The background is always kept in long shot, even when the subject moves into close up. Fortunately, in close-ups, when depth of field is most restricted, its importance also decreases. It is natural to have a rather unsharp background when looking at nearby objects. But in long shot both subject and background are normally expected to be sharp.

Projector Focal Length

Shortage of studio space can influence the arrangement of back projection. If a 20-ft screen is used in a small studio and the projector may only be taken back 50 ft, a wide-angle lens is needed on the projector to cover the screen. This could give rise to a bright spot in the centre of the screen, the image falling off in intensity toward the edges. In a larger studio the camera could be moved farther away and a longer focus lens used to give a much more even spread of light over the screen. The bright centre only occurs when the projector is too close to the screen. It is not good practice to use the projector in this way. If there is no alternative, a hot spot filter must be placed in the light path between projector and screen to lessen the intensity only at the centre. It consists of a circular neutral density screen suspended from cottons, and has to be adjusted to the correct position.

It is advisable to use longer focus lenses on the projector where possible. The focal length of lens used and movement of the projector affect the brightness of the image thrown onto the screen. With a long shot the maximum light output is needed from the projector. The smaller screen picture used for medium shots and close-ups is much more brilliant and so the projector output may be dropped accordingly. On the other hand when the camera moves forward the advantage of a brighter picture means that a smaller aperture can be used, say, $f\,5.6$ instead of $f\,4.5$, for greater depth. Because of that extra light on the screen the studio lighting must be stepped up to match and so maintain a correct balance of light on foreground and background.

Car Interiors

An example where a wide-angle lens has to be used on the camera for a back projection scene is a car interior with four people, which might show the driver with his hands on the wheel, a passenger next to him and two other people in the back seat. A wide-angle lens gives enough depth to include front and back passengers and the close view provides the perspective which allows all four people to be seen. If they were shot from farther away with a long focus lens it would be extremely difficult to see past the front people and obtain a good view of those in the back, and, at the same time, hold them all sharp. A long focus lens has so little depth of field.

Several things have to be rehearsed in a car mock-up scene. As well as being vibrated on its rockers, the mock-up may be moved to one side or another when the car turns a corner. As the back projection swings round, two stage hands can give it the appropriate lean. At the same time, the key light might have to be moved so that the angle of the sunlight falling on the occupants appears to change as it would in the real scene.

The screen image, as well as appearing to turn a corner, will show a change of lighting, say, from frontal to side lighting, and the studio lights must be moved to coincide exactly with this. These light changes are particularly noticeable on the actors in the foreground.

Another plate might represent a view from the back of a car running along a country road and suddenly passing a line of trees where the shadow of the trees covers the road. Corresponding shadows must be made to pass over the actors in the foreground to give the impression that they are actually going under the trees. Several studio men with pieces of twig attached to sticks could pass them across the key lights to throw dappled shadows. A row of telegraph poles at the side of the road could be simulated by passing a single shadow from a stick over the same light at regular intervals. Without these effects, the subject does not look as if it really belongs to the background and the illusion is destroyed.

FRONT PROJECTION

Front projection is a process used for combining live studio action with a projected background, which may be animated or static. The process uses a special background screen which has a glass-beaded surface with highly directional reflection characteristics. This is positioned behind the actor and facing the camera. In front of the camera is a semi reflecting (pellicle) mirror angled horizontally at 45°. The camera shoots through this mirror. A projector containing the still or moving "plate" is positioned to one side of the camera with its optical axis at right angles to that of the camera lens. The projector and camera shutters are synchronized. The projected image falls on the surface of the mirror and is reflected on to the directional screen. The camera films the actor and the projected image combined. The actor's shadow on the screen is exactly masked by his own body as seen from the camera position directly along the optical axis it shares with the projector.

The image from the screen is exceptionally bright even without a particularly powerful projector because the special "reflex" screen surface has the characteristic of reflecting almost all the light directly back along the path of its incidence. The actor's face, being, in these terms, a relatively inefficient reflector, shows only very weakly the portion of the projected image falling on it—indeed the process depends

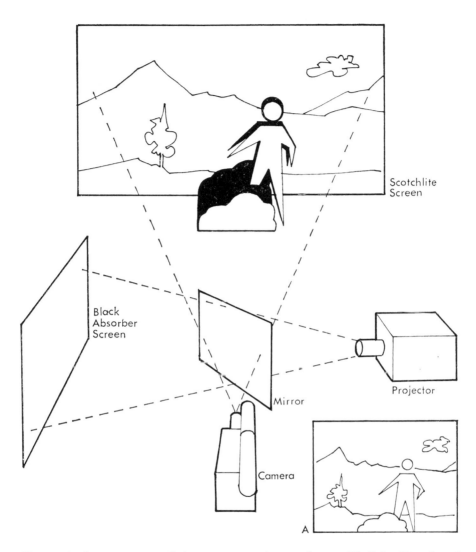

Front projection arrangement of mirror, camera, projector and screen. The "plate" is projected onto a Scotchlite screen via the reflecting surface of a semi-silvered mirror, pieces of screen being attached to cut shapes corresponding with any foreground features the actor is to move behind. A black screen absorbs any transmitted light that might otherwise be reflected back onto the reverse side of the mirror and so into the camera lens. The camera, set up along the axis of the projector beam shoots through the semi-silvered mirror recording the scene as shown at A.

on a substantial difference in brightness between this image and the one reflected from the screen. The image on the face is in any case easily eliminated by subsequent lighting which, though kept reasonably clear from the screen would not interfere with the highly directional projected image. Theoretically, any stray light, hitting the screen would be returned directly along the axis of the light-emitting source.

It is possible to cut out sections of the "Scotchlite" reflecting screen and position them forward of the normal screen position matching a feature in the projected image, so that the actor may appear to pass *behind* the feature or prop seen in the "plate." By arranging the reflective material on the floor in strips facing the camera it is possible to show the actor walking about in the projected scene on the projected "ground." The Scotchlite reflective material is supplied in rolls 2 ft wide and may be papered (preferably combining rolls from the same batch to ensure uniformity of reflectance) with overlapping joins onto any surface. The surface need not be completely even nor be absolutly flat onto the camera.

It is important that the camera, projector and mirror should be properly aligned and the mirror kept free from flare or extraneous light. To avoid a secondary image from the percentage of projector light *transmitted* by the semi-silvered mirror being picked up from its rear surface the projector images passing through the mirror are arranged to fall on a small black absorbent surface facing the projector.

Alignment can be checked by looking through the lens on the camera; any error will show as a fringe round the actor's body and great care must be taken with alignment when shooting a moving actor; the scene can be checked during rehearsals. Generally, the whole of the projected image is included in the shot. If a smaller part of the image (itself usually a positive print from a negative original) is made to fill the background there will be a severe loss of image quality due to grain, besides of course a possible over-enlargement of background features, which will make the effect far less convincing. If, on the other hand, the plate is reduced to fill a small part of the picture this reduction of the relative size of the projected image will tend to enhance its quality.

The advantages of front projection are the smaller studio space required than with back projection (page 216), a projector light source of more modest power, good image quality, greater operational freedom in the placing of actors and lighting, and the scope for depth effects with features in the projected plate being projected on foreground areas treated with reflex screen. Moreover, with front projection the background screen may be of very large size without causing illumination problems.

Against this there is some restriction in the movement of actors and total restriction on camera movement.

10

Marine Sequences

MARINE SEQUENCES CAN involve a very full range of camera and lighting techniques because of the many forms they take—mostly with the added nuisance-factor of the water itself. The crew might be working on a real ship at sea shooting from a static platform, or, in a different situation, they may have to set up the camera *in* the water. The ship could be a full-scale mock-up in a specially flooded studio, or a scale model floating in a tank on the studio lot, perhaps with an artificial background. The sequence might have to convey the mood of halcyon days or the turmoil of a tropical storm and the shots may have to show only a ship or they might involve live actors.

Below are set out some of the marine sequence situations more frequently met with on large-scale productions, and methods suggested for shooting them.

SHIPS—CAMERA VIEWPOINT AND EXPOSURE

Where the actors are seen in a small boat from a nearby viewpoint the camera could be set up in another boat lashed to it alongside. If it had to be far enough away to show the whole boat the shots could be taken from a low barge, which is an ideal vessel for such a shot because it combines relative stability with the option of a low viewpoint. For a scene to be acted out in a small boat, the low viewpoint is the basic one and the most used.

Exposures for each camera in a multi-camera set-up are decided by the director of photography and he calls them out to the respective operators. The initial reading may be taken from the sun or the face of a nearby person and a balance worked out from these two. He then decides the settings for the various cameras which, being at different positions, with various angles of view might need different exposures. The reason is simple. A camera between decks might be shutting out half the sky from the picture, while another with the lens set for a close view may see no sky at all.

The view least affected by ship movement is probably that from the camera with a wide-angle lens. The close shots with a long focus lens may have to contend with greater variations in this respect. In a sweep shot going from a low to a highly lit subject where no exposure adjustment is possible, the director of photography reads high and low levels and sets the lens between the two. He keeps his operators posted of exposures all the time.

It is far easier to do a calm sea sequence in the studio than a storm. A painted sky backing when properly lit looks very realistic. Naturally, the calm sea also avoids the need for the many extra effects required for a storm. The feeling of a ship riding on a slight swell can be conveyed by gentle movement of the camera, up and down and back and forth. The camera can be mounted on a crane, and if on two heads, it can also be slowly tilted from side to side. This movement has to be varied with the shooting direction and the way the ship is supposed to be rolling.

The painted sky backing includes the distant horizon, glimpsed from time to time as it rises and falls in the lower part of the picture. Actors, too, have to simulate the sway. As the camera moves one way they sway the other, against it always. This must be rehearsed. They would not do it all the time, but only in certain shots where it is needed.

Studio Storms—Protecting the Camera

In a studio storm sequence the camera is protected from water by a tarpaulin but, despite that, the lens is often covered with spray. A certain amount of spray has no effect on the picture, but the lens should be wiped, all the same, at the end of each take. A greater nuisance is that the combination of damp atmosphere and warm studio put condensation on and in the lens. With heavy condensation and with much water flying about the whole camera can become wet, and must be taken off the stage to be warmed and dried in the camera room. The lens cannot be protected with a glass while shooting. A few spots would show where they would not show on the lens itself. It is best to keep the camera covered during the rehearsals of actors and effects.*

Lighting units are affected by dampness and water droplets.

* High-speed revolving glass screens such as those used on the bridge of ocean-going vessels are available for motion picture purposes and, attached to waterproof camera covers, efficiently solve the problem of unwanted spray on the lens. This combination was developed by the camera crew on *Ryan's Daughter* for use on the storm sequence and has now become a standard item of equipment which can be hired from Samuelson Film Service.

Bubbles (lamp bulbs) blow most frequently, but arcs can be trouble-some if a considerable amount of water gets onto them.

SEA FILM LOCATIONS

When choosing the location, it is wise to select a place sufficiently far away from the land so that the camera can be used in various directions without the bother of land in the background. On the other hand, it should not, for the sake of convenience, be too far out. It can be a tremendous waste of time bringing the unit out every day from a land base. It might be necessary to think in terms of chartering a ship.

The location should be far out enough to give the impression of deep sea if it is meant to be. But choice of location is also directly connected with the weather needed in the film—the Mediterranean is an obvious place for sunny weather—and the west coast of Ireland for heavy seas and overcast conditions. Where the background must represent another country an uncharacteristic part of the local coast-line might serve the purpose. For a production team working in England, the coast of Cornwall could convincingly represent a foreign country.

SHIPS—ACTION AND SLOW MOTION

When shooting a sailing ship at sea to give an impression of speed, the camera can be undercranked—run below normal speed—so that on projection the action is accelerated. A shooting speed of 16 or 18 fps would give the desired effect but a watch must be kept for details in the action that would spoil the effect. A too-rapidly flapping sail can look ridiculous.

The amount of extra speed allowable also depends on the shooting angle. If the ship is moving toward the camera, the sequence can be speeded up considerably. But the effect of speed alteration shows much more where the ship is seen sideways on.

For slow motion, speeds of 32, 48, 72 and 96 fps are used, depending on the desired effect and the apparent speed of the subject. For full slow motion, where the camera needs to be run at up to four times normal speed (i.e. 96 fps) a specially designed high-speed camera should be used. Higher speeds need other types of special camera, some designed to take up to 100,000 fps or more.

STUDIO AND OUTDOOR SEA SEQUENCES

A full-scale ship or the section of it needed for a film can be con-structed in the studio or out on a studio lot. It might be built on stilts, high enough to exclude the surrounding landscape from near-level shots and to fill the background with sky only. Or it may be set up in an outside tank with a large painted sky backing.

Disadvantages with working on an outdoor set are apparent if extensive night storm sequences are needed requiring two or three weeks' work—because work can only be carried out at night. In mid-winter working conditions are too harsh for throwing water or immersing actors or stuntmen and outdoor tanks are therefore used mainly for models or perhaps for a short water sequence. A studio can be kept reasonably warm, and in any case it affords more control over conditions.

The backing on an outdoor set is a fairly solid assembly to resist movement in the wind, it is positioned at one end of the outdoor tank and is sometimes tilted slightly upwards to gather the maximum light from the sky. The outdoor set-up has a special advantage for shooting models needing a four times normal camera speed to obtain realistic movement of the water. If the ship is one-quarter scale, it has to be shot, theoretically speaking, at four times the speed (i.e. slow motion) for wave movement correct for a wave of four times the size. When shooting at these speeds strong sunshine is a help with exposure. A tremendous amount of light is needed to film this kind of effect in the studio.

While the backing on an outdoor tank covers one end only, that in the studio can, if required, extend all the way round. It need be no more substantial than canvas as there is, of course, no wind and seldom any artificially produced air turbulence directed at it.

STORMS AT SEA

The typical storm-at-sea sequence is sometimes manufactured in the studio, which provides the necessary control. It is usually set up in a large tank and a large stage at a studio like the silent stage at Shepperton which can be flooded to a suitable depth, say, 4 ft 6 in. This provides watery accommodation for a full-scale ship 200 ft long, with its sides rising 10 ft above water level. The ship rests on rockers so that it can roll from side to side.*

Although the ship might fill the entire stage with only a few feet to spare at either end this is enough for movement in a storm sequence. Full rain, wave, lightning and wind effects can then be introduced. Rain can be provided by overhead pipes, and heavy waves to wash over

* A full-size ship built in the studio has movable sections, like a house interior set. Parts of the superstructure, for example, may be struck for certain scenes, and the delay in doing this may be two to three hours, a wastage that is allowed for in advance. As with the interior set, it should be possible to make good the altered section for a later scene.

the decks can be tipped in from large tanks suspended just outside the picture. Wave machines operate in the tank to make the water rough, and wind is blown across the whole scene to add to the effect. Intermittent lightning flashes are also introduced. Fog too, may be needed when, the following morning, the sea is calm and the dawn comes up.

For long shots of the ship at sea in the same simulated weather conditions a scale model can be shot in the same tank. If it is a night scene there is no problem in producing enough light for the high filming speeds needed for model shots.

All technical people taking part need substantial waterproof clothing for this operation.

SHIP-MOVEMENT EFFECT

To gain the maximum effect of movement in shipboard scenes with a heaving deck the camera should not itself be on the deck but mounted separately on the arm of a crane. A camera on the deck minimizes the action. In a scene where someone is tied to the wheel and water is swirling about and streaming across the deck it conflicts with the objectives of the scene. The separate, static camera intensifies the relative movement.

In daylight, with some background visible, the sway of the boat can be clearly seen. But in a night scene with only a black background, the movement can only be shown by the movement of the vessel between the static camera and background. The usual background is a large canvas backing about 40 ft high and going all round the studio leaving only an opening for the door. This background cannot move, although it is just about possible, if the boat does not move, to throw a shadow "horizon" onto it with a suitable masked lamp. The mask has a movable lower flap throwing a fairly well-defined line onto the background. This is a night backing, and the feeling is given of tilting back and forth against the dark ocean, which is simply a dark grey-blue shadow at the bottom of the backing. This method is used only where there are not enough funds to build a ship on rockers. To place a large ship on rockers is a major construction job involving the installation of hydraulic lifts. Hydraulic engineers have to be brought in specially for the job and it can add several thousand pounds to the production bill.

Some economies can be made in building the ship itself if only one side is needed. For a single day's work only a small section may be required. But a ship on which several weeks of work are to be done should be a complete representation with correct details going all the way round and all over so that shooting can take place in every direction.

Models—Shooting Schedule

The scale model shooting programme is organized according to the importance of the scene in the film and any special technical difficulties involved.

If a model is to be filmed without involving actors, a second unit working with the special effects department would probably tackle it. But the project would be done under the surveillance of the chief cameraman and the director of the film. A complex scene such as a sea battle at dawn, with the special lighting this requires should be shot by the director of photography. If he has a good man working under him, many model shots might be left more or less to him. Although working on his own, he would carry out instructions given him by the director which he would also discuss with the lighting cameraman so that a continuity of lighting would be maintained.

A section of the film involving two or three weeks of work with models might be more economically done with a second unit, while the first continues on material involving the actors. The acted scenes in most films are nearly always the most important, particularly where stars are involved. If the model work is enough for only one day the cameraman would probably do this with the director. Only when there is a sizeable slice of model shooting is it farmed out to a second unit. The director sees their rushes each day and either passes them or has them re-shot to his satisfaction.

Scale Models

The length of time that a model shot appears in the final film often depends on the realism. For lengthy sequences, absolute realism is of course of fundamental importance. But many model shots are intended as little more than snippets to support the illusion of a chain of events. Even for a brief few seconds' flash, considerable efforts are made to get a realistic result, and repeated takes are common in this type of work.

Rubber dolls dressed for the part are frequently used in ship models to line the deck. As they are made to sway about, seen in short flashes from some distance they can be quite convincing.

A more elaborate model in which some men are seen rowing a boat can be successful for brief shots provided they are photographed in the right way. They are usually inter-cut with close shots of the same subject, and the ability to convince the audience that the models are the real thing has much to do also with the action in the sequence being continuous.

The model boat in which the dolls must move might be at a

reasonable scale, if it were 6 ft long, the dolls being 1 ft high each. The oars are driven by a small electric motor in the boat which produces the correct to-and-fro strokes. The dolls' hands are fixed to the oars and bend with them. The boat rows the men rather than the other way round. Such a boat, being tossed about in the water, might be filmed at three times normal speed. Seen through a rain effect and lit to the best advantage, the whole impression can be realistic enough for several seconds' screen time.

Sea Location Work

It is standard practice when filming at sea to screw the camera down on a platform which is fastened to the deck of the ship. Very often, although the scene is shot at sea, the scenes demand as steady a camera as possible. This seems at first sight to be a waste of the natural environment. Actually, many sea sequences in which a boat is to be photographed are specifically written with the concept of isolation, loneliness and the vastness of the ocean as the dominant dramatic theme. To convey this feeling of isolation the scenes must not *seem* to have been shot from another craft, whereas in a race sequence at sea, for example, violent camera movement would be quite natural if it were supposed to represent the view from one ship to another.

If the camera is significantly influenced by the movement of the boat it is mounted on, the audience feel as if they, too, are on board ship. To avoid this impression the operator has to counteract the rocking of the boat as best he can by a gentle movement of the pan and tilt head. There is of course bound to be some movement, but it is unlikely to become distracting.

A large boat is a stable shooting platform and such a boat can provide a working base for perhaps fifty people working on the picture —director, continuity girl, camera team, sound, actors, props, etc. A team as large as this can be needed even when the subject of the film is only a rowing boat.

For the film *Lord Jim* various kinds of boat material were used —mostly filmed in Hong Kong harbour. A large barge was hired for the occasion and, as it had no engine of its own, it was roped to a powerful tugboat. Many types of boat were photographed from this barge. The camera, sound, lamps and crew were on board and a generator provided current for a couple of brutes. Reflectors were also used. An iron overslung platform was constructed to suspend from the barge over the water so that the camera, placed on the end of it, could be just a few inches above sea level. The cage on the end was actually sunk in the water, so the legs of the tripod supporting the camera in the cage were also submerged.

This was ideal for getting low-level shots of people in rowing boats where they were perhaps only 2 ft 6 in. above water level. The barge, being independent from the tugboat though steered by the ropes, lost the vibration of the tugboat's engines, and when towed at some distance behind the tugboat it also lost the engine noise.

The work of a motion picture cameraman, and, in fact, feature film production in a larger context involves both technical and artistic elements which are completely interdependent. Although the camera-man and various other personnel are normally regarded as artists, it is not always realized that this artistry must rest on secure technical foundations. For a proper harmony between these aspects it is essential if anything worthwhile, let alone outstanding, is to be achieved in a medium which demands so many skills.

Glossary

ANTI-FLARE TREATMENT. Spray used on highly reflecting surfaces to reduce flare.

BARN DOORS. Hinged flaps mounted on the rim or lens of a lamp which can be opened or closed independently to control the shape of the light beam or shade off spill light.

BREAKDOWN (SCRIPT). Analysis of film script in terms of scenes with the same locations, sets, properties, etc., which are then filmed together and rearranged in correct sequential order at the editing stage.

CAMERA GRIP. Stage hand attached to the camera crew of a film unit whose duties include moving the dolly or camera crane and removing or carrying equipment.

CENTURY STAND. General-purpose wheeled stand used around the studio mainly for holding small props or apparatus used in lighting effects.

CLAPPER BOARD. A board with two parts, joined by a hinge, which are clapped together at the start or end of a dialogue sequence to provide a sync reference point for sound and picture. Many present-day recording systems have dispensed with this method.

COLOUR CONVERSION FILTER. Filtering material placed over lens, lamp or window to adjust the colour temperature of light in the scene to suit the colour balance of a particular stock in the camera.

COLOUR CORRECTION (OR COMPENSATING) FILTER. A filter placed over the camera lens to make subtle adjustments to the colour quality in the scene, e.g. to slightly accentuate the red content of evening light, or perhaps to reduce that effect so that the scene more closely matches others shot earlier in the day.

COLOUR TEMPERATURE. The temperature in degrees Celsius measured from absolute zero by which a theoretical black body (i.e. a perfect radiator which is totally absorbent of incident radiation) must be raised in order to radiate light of a certain quality. Colour temperature is measured in Kelvins, the higher temperatures (bluer light) having the higher figure, the lower (pinkish) having the lower.

COOKIE. A patterned cut-out in a flag, or irregular shape supported on a stand in the same way as a flag and placed in the light path to throw a soft or hard pattern or shape on the scene.

CUTAWAY. A shot of something other than the main action. A cutaway is inserted between shots of the main action, often to bridge a lapse in time or to avoid an unwanted jump cut.

DUBBING. The process of combining several sound recordings on separate tracks to make one final mixed soundtrack. Also the term given to revoicing a film in another language.

FILLER LIGHT (ALSO FILL OR FILL-IN LIGHT). A light used to raise the level of shadow illumination and so reduce the overall contrast of a scene.

FLAG. Rectangular piece of wood or card of small size attached to a staff and mounted on a studio stand and adjusted to prevent stray light entering the camera lens, or, when placed in a light beam, to shade off a part of the set.

FLOATING WALL. A wall in a set which is designed for removal when the space is required for certain camera angles or movements.

FOOT LAMBERT. Unit of luminance describing the brightness of a perfectly diffusing surface when the light falling equals 1 foot-candle (one lumen per square foot). Applied in cinematography to reflective readings taken from the subject.

FOOT-CANDLE. Unit of illumination, light intensity at a surface 1 ft away from a standard candle (literally at the surface of a sphere of 1 ft radius with the candle at its centre). It is equal to one lumen per square foot. In cinematography, applied to incident readings of lamps from the subject position.

GAFFER. Senior electrician in a film unit. He ensures that the correct number of lamps of the right power (and associated equipment including generators where needed) are available to the cameraman for each set-up. He instructs electricians in the placing and movement, if any, of the lamps for the shot, as required by the cameraman.

GLASS SHOT. Special effect where a section of the scene is painted on a glass sheet and placed in front of the lens so that when photographed it appears to be a part of the set, thus avoiding the need for expensive construction in that area.

GOBO. Large black-painted wooden screen or mask supported by a low stand and used to shield the lens from unwanted light, or shade off certain parts of the set.

HEADROOM. In composition the space between the top of an object being photographed and the top of the frame.

KELVIN. Scale of units applied to the measurement of colour temperature (colour quality of a light source), and based on degrees Celsius measured from absolute zero ($-273°C$).

LOCATION. Outdoor site (beyond the studio lot) where shooting takes place.

LOT. Outdoor studio area where filming takes place and elaborate scenery can be erected or effects staged.

MATTE SHOT. Shot in which part of the scene is obscured by a cut-out mask or metal sheet placed in front of the lens.

N.G. TAKE. An unsuccessful take. Literally "No Good" take.

PACE. In its simplest form the speeding up or lengthening of a sequence by mechanically shortening or extending each scene or image but normally applied to the relationship between the length of each shot and the events it shows, and their effect in the sequence as a whole.

PAN. Pivotal movement of the camera on a horizontal plane.

PAN GLASS. A filter glass for observing the scene before shooting. It converts the sensitivity of the eye to that of a panchromatic emulsion. It may be used with other filters, especially contrast filters, for judging the photographic effect. Another type, the monochromatic vision filter eliminates all colour differences leaving only differences in brightness. A true monochromatic effect is thus obtained.

PUP. A 500- or 750-W focusing spot lamp to which barn doors, snoot or filters can be attached.

RUSHES (OR DAILIES). First (and ungraded) positive prints made by a laboratory from the material photographed on the previous day. Only certain takes are printed and these are viewed each day by the producer and main crew members so that any retakes can be carried out before the set is struck

SET-UP. Refers to the position of the camera, and what is seen in the viewfinder. Also means the act of mounting the camera or laying tracks and positioning the dolly.

SHUTTER CONTROL. Device whereby the camera shutter opening can be increased or decreased by adjusting the size of the shutter blade. This provides extra control over the amount of light reaching the film apart from by a change of aperture, which in certain circumstances may not be desirable. Shutter angle is the size of the open segment which, fully open, could be 180° so that half open is 90° and quarter open 45°. Most 35-mm cameras have a maximum shutter angle of 170–180°.

SNOOT. A shade, usually tubular in shape, which, when fitted onto the front of a lamp, confines the light beam to a smaller area.

STRIKE (SET). Dismantling a set to make room for another.

TILT. Pivotal camera movement in a vertical plane. Special tripod heads provide for extreme angles of tilt with a counterbalancing or wedge device to prevent the camera from falling over.

WIND MACHINE. A machine for blowing air for wind effects. A large 4-speed model is for blowing rain and smaller versions are designed for blowing air.

Index